Cultivating Positive Minds:
Behavior Support in Indian Education

Dr. Naidu Sanjay R.

BLUEROSE PUBLISHERS
India | U.K.

Copyright © Dr. Naidu Sanjay R. 2025

All rights reserved by author. No part of this publication may be reproduced, stored in a retrieval system or transmitted in any form or by any means, electronic, mechanical, photocopying, recording or otherwise, without the prior permission of the author. Although every precaution has been taken to verify the accuracy of the information contained herein, the publisher assumes no responsibility for any errors or omissions. No liability is assumed for damages that may result from the use of information contained within.

BlueRose Publishers takes no responsibility for any damages, losses, or liabilities that may arise from the use or misuse of the information, products, or services provided in this publication.

For permissions requests or inquiries regarding this publication, please contact:

BLUEROSE PUBLISHERS
www.BlueRoseONE.com
info@bluerosepublishers.com
+91 8882 898 898
+4407342408967

ISBN: 978-93-6783-650-7

Cover Design: Aman Sharma
Typesetting: Pooja Sharma

First Edition: April 2025

Acknowledgement

Writing this book has been an incredible journey, one that would not have been possible without the unwavering support and encouragement of the people who have stood by me through every step of the way.

First and foremost, I would like to express my heartfelt gratitude to my mother, Vijaya, for her unconditional love and guidance, which have been my constant source of strength. I deeply cherish the values instilled in me by my late father, Rajaram, whose memory continues to inspire me to strive for excellence in all that I do.

I am profoundly grateful to my brothers, Sunil and Vishal, for their encouragement and belief in me, which motivated me to persevere through challenges. My spouse, Vijayshree, has been my pillar of support, offering immense patience, understanding, and motivation during the course of this work. I am equally thankful to my daughter, Shraddha, and my son, Shivam, My brother son Satyam for their love, support, and the joy they bring into my life, which keeps me grounded and focused.

I also extend my sincere gratitude to Dr.Radhika Inamdar and Dr. Dipak Chavan, who introduced me to this subject and guided me towards pursuing it as a topic of research.

To all these incredible individuals, this book stands as a testament to their contributions and belief in my capabilities. I am forever indebted to them for their unwavering support.

With Gratitude:

My Mother - My Strength
Smt. Vijaya Rajaram Naidu

My Father - My Hero.
Late Shri Rajaram Keshav Naidu

Preface

Positive Behaviour Support (PBS) is a framework that emphasises the creation of supportive environments where individuals are guided to thrive through encouragement, respect, and shared values. When we look to history for inspiration in leadership and community building, one figure stands out for embodying these principles long before they were formally articulated: Chatrapati Shivaji Maharaj. His legacy of leadership, rooted in inclusivity, discipline, and support for his people, offers timeless lessons on fostering positive behaviour, whether in governance, society, or education.

Throughout history we come across living characters who upheld certain values and practised such strategies which are relevant even after centuries. They can be taken up as reference to forge our way through the rough waves of modernism and the challenging task of raising and building young minds. In the annals of history one such dynamic character is that of the Maratha king, Chatrapati Shivaji Maharaj whose leadership principles and strategies are exemplary to this day in their appeal. Chatrapati Shivaji Maharaj appeared at such a time in the horizon of Indian history when the country's ethnicity was facing one of those turbulent times and Chatrapati Shivaji Maharaj became the symbol of hope for the countrymen, fighting the war to keep their essence alive against the adverse forces. The championing presence of Chatrapati Shivaji Maharaj in the crossroads of Indian history throws light on the importance of a supportive and disciplined environment in every aspect of progress, either educational or societal.

When examined closely it can be noted that the greatest weapon of this Maratha king was the unwavering support of his countrymen in his way of building the most formidable empire in history. Faced with external threats and internal divisions, he built an empire not just with military strength but through a deep understanding of human values and the need for collective unity. His leadership was anchored in creating an environment where individuals were motivated, valued, and given the responsibility to contribute to a common cause. These traits align remarkably with the core elements of PBS, which seeks to empower individuals through positive reinforcement, respect, and accountability. The rich tapestry of Chatrapati Shivaji's ruling policy was adorned by the strategies that can be called his thoughtful leadership and positive behaviour support as a building blocks of the thriving community. His strategies were more modern and farsighted and thus they have earned their place in this book which will delve deep into the exploration of positive behaviour support in the modern education system through the framework of the great Maratha king.

In the era which upheld the stigma of social division as a thriving force Chatrapati Shivaji Maharaj brought the strategies of inclusivity. To foster the sense of unity within diversity he included men from different religious and social backgrounds, omitting the hindering cultural barriers and opening the doors to all to create a community of harmony to stand tall against the intruders. He realised that at the end of the day the common goal of each Maratha man should be one and they must strive with collective responsibility. A common goal and working towards it without any narrowness of the minds is the first lesson he tried to foster in the minds of his people and the impact became history. Similarly, PBS thrives on the idea of creating environments where everyone, regardless of their background, feels supported and encouraged to reach their full potential.

Once he successfully broke the barriers he realised the need for delegation and thus brought in the concept of shared authority in the field of decision making. It created the much needed trust among local leaders. The famous " Ashta Pradhan" or Council of Eight Ministers further strengthened his view when local leaders were allowed to take charge of their respective domains and to check their limits they were also held responsible and accountable for any decision they made. This can be considered as the early example of a leadership role to build the firmness of character. Chatrapati Shivaji Maharaj used this tool not only for the bigger goal but also for the personal growth of men to become self disciplined in their way to become potential future leaders. This mirrors PBS's emphasis on clear expectations, where positive behaviour is reinforced through guidance and feedback, ensuring that individuals feel both valued and responsible for their actions.

Chatrapati Shivaji Maharaj acknowledged the talents and skills and not the ranks of their birth and caste and rewarded the worthy individuals their due respect and acknowledgement. By elevating individuals for their talents not for their background he stimulated motivation in them and a zeal to do even better. It was a culture of excellence that he weaved, where a little elevation paved the way for future excellence positively. He realised that the people who are with him needed to be valued for their roles within a well disciplined structure. He valued his people, showed them empathy for their families as well but all this happened under the well knitted tapestry of strict disciples that maintained the order in a balanced manner. PBS, too, upholds the importance of rewards and encouragement as a source of motivation.

However all these strategies are not just applicable on his subjects but he believed that for imbibing these values into his people he needed to create an example in himself and thus we today have him as the most venerated and admired leader of history who was the personification of bravery, chivalry and ethics. Even in the battlefield he never wavered from his values and ethics, setting a strong example for his people and future leaders to follow. He maintained the moral compass in every challenging circumstance showcasing the value of integrity as the backbone of any man. Chatrapati Shivaji Maharaj fought along his soldiers as a way of showing them his respect. In his battles or in his aspirations he never lost the touch of humility and made sure that his people understood that he valued their service. The kindness and emotional strength he showed to his fellow men reverberated through their devotion and loyalty for him. This kind of leadership is crucial in Positive Behaviour Support, where leaders and educators model the behaviour they wish to see, providing a framework of consistency and moral clarity for those they guide.

In Chatrapati Shivaji Maharaj's story, we find a remarkable model of leadership that aligns with the principles of Positive Behaviour Support. His ability to foster unity, build trust, and encourage personal growth resonates deeply with the ideals of PBS. This book seeks to explore and draw from these historical lessons, applying them to the modern context of education and behavioural support. Just as Chatrapati Shivaji Maharaj empowered his people to achieve greatness through mutual respect and support, so too can PBS empower individuals to succeed in environments that promote positive, respectful, and responsible behaviour.These strategies, taken up by Chatrapati Shivaji Maharaj, are not just mere facts of history but they are the guidance of the past, a flickering light of wisdom in the gloom of modern life. Looking back doesn't mean a failure of progression. Looking back at times is the way to gain insight and the strategies of positive behaviour practised by Chatrapati Shivaji Maharaj are like those insights that will allow us to build a positive environment for the blooming minds of our country to push them towards a brighter future wherein they will carry their country along with them. As we delve into the strategies and philosophies of Positive Behaviour Support, we will draw from Chatrapati Shivaji Maharaj's timeless example, exploring how the values he championed can continue to inspire and shape the way we create supportive, inclusive, and nurturing environments today.

Contents

Chapter-1: Introduction to Positive Behaviour System in Schools 1

Chapter-2: Role of Culture and Values in Shaping Behaviour 11

Chapter-4: Core Principles of Positive Behaviour Support . 29

Chapter-5: PBS and Family Engagement 38

Chapter-6: A Positive School-wide Positive Behaviour Support Framework 47

Chapter-7: Positive Behaviour Support Strategies for Classrooms 56

Chapter-8: Role of Teachers in Positive Behaviour Support 66

Chapter-9: Applying Positive Behaviour Support for Challenging Behaviors and Special Students 76

Conclusion 98

About the Author 100

Chapter-1: Introduction to Positive Behaviour System in Schools

For any student, only academic development is not enough. The ultimate growth of a student depends on the social, emotional and academic success and to promote such tiered development the most effective framework is the Positive Development System. As discussed in the preface, the Positive Behaviour System is not a new innovation. It has been indirectly regulating behaviour since the time of the great leader Chatrapati Shivaji Maharaj. The great Maratha king had won the loyalty of his clan and even to this day he has been an exemplary figure of honour and reverence due to the strategic system of influencing the behaviour of his people in the times of swaraj crisis. But in recent times there aren't any threats of external invasion. Today the challenge lies in building a positive system to ensure the behavioural development of the young minds, precisely the students. With a focus on the proactive strategies, PBS aims at creating a more learner friendly, inclusive, and supportive learning environment for young students while constantly addressing and correcting the disruptive traits of behaviours. This responsibility lies with the guidance of the teachers and parents and their innovative system to reinforce positive behaviour and rectify the unwanted ones more strategically. As a leading expert in PBS believed, "The key to successful behaviour support is teaching and reinforcing expected behaviours rather than simply punishing unwanted ones."

As Dr. Robert Horner has observed, PBS is not just another way of classroom control; rather the goal and effect of such a system has a bigger prospect outside the boundary of schools. PBS teaches skills like communication, leadership, teamwork, and empathy which are like stepping stones in the social development of a child. Moreover PBS sets out clear expectations, enabling the students to become more responsible for their actions. Therefore PBS is a unifying support system that can be collaboratively achieved by the parents, guardians or teachers and it is a system which ensures the personal growth of a student and the success of the school community at large.

The Universal Approach of Positive Behaviour System on Schools:

A robust Positive Behaviour system not only enhances learning outcomes of a student but ensures and prepares for future success. There is a universal appeal to the PBS and as a proactive approach to behaviour management also enhances the entire school community with a culture of respect and responsibility.

1. Enhanced Learning Environment

In a classroom PBS creates a positive learning environment. A positive learning environment means a place where the student feels safe and supported which in the long run helps in their academic success. To create such a positive environment the teachers are needed to establish a clear set of rules, constituted of respect, empathy and responsibility. Through positive reinforcement of these values through praise students will eventually feel a sense of belonging and will engage them more in the learning process.

2. Improved Student Behaviour

The biggest goal of PBS is reducing disruptive behaviours and promoting a positive one. If a school implements such a system where students are rewarded with extra points for their behaviours such as helping peers and collaboration, such an effort will foster motivation in students. If schools successfully and consistently maintain this reinforcement process, soon the students will learn what kind of behaviour is expected from them and will create a more productive classroom dynamic.

3. Skill Development

In order to conduct the PBS it is pertinent to make the students face the real-life situations to know and understand the behaviours they need to showcase and practice. This is crucial for developing their social and emotional skills. Through role playing methods, if students participate in real life disagreements and other crises they will know about the application of the positive behaviours that they have learned. This method allows them achieve better interpersonal relationships and an all over future success.

4. Support for Diverse Needs

PBS is the most efficient way of realising the diverse needs of students and the different levels of support that they need. In a school students with different issues like interactive limitations can be dealt with strategically with the help of social skill groups where interactive activities will structurally help them to overcome the issue. Personalised tailored structures often prove beneficial in curing such issues at an early age.

5. Collaboration and Community Involvement

PBS promotes a collaboration among educators, families and community to unified approach to behaviour management. When a school conducts workshops for parents to educate them on PBS they can reinforce positive behaviours at home. In this way the PBS does not stay limited to schools and involves families and communities as well, if the school teaches the positive behaviours those behaviours get reinforced at home by parents.

6. Reduction in Disciplinary Actions

By implementing PBS at school actively disciplinary actions such as suspensions and expulsions can be reduced. In a school if the students misbehave the authority can take restorative practices instead of the immediate punitive measures. By PBS students can be made to reflect on their behaviour and participate in a discussion to rectify and prevent such events in the future. So in a way PBS ensures that students are supported at all stages.

7. Empowerment of Students

The most interesting aspect of PBS is that it offer the students a voice and chance to be involved in the behaviour management process wherein they understand the rules and expectations and learn to take responsibility for their behaviour. By participating in discussions and brainstorming they contribute in creating the ideal environment of the classroom. This helps in the characteristic growth of students by encouraging them to be accountable for their actions in a supportive way.

Though PBS has originated from the need to address the challenges of behaviours in schools, recently PBS is a proof that behaviour can be taught, reinforced, and modified through a strategic effort. In the past few decades PBS has evolved significantly and has also evolved not only as theory but as an applicable framework to regulate and monitor students' behaviour. PBS takes its modern shape from the Applied Behaviour Analysis (ABA). ABA is a scientific approach to identify the principles of behaviour and improve socially acceptable behaviour. It mainly focuses on the understanding of the functions of behaviour and by providing educators and teachers evidence based strategies it helps them in reinforcing positive behaviour, effectively addressing challenging behaviour and setting a clear list of expectations. This foundation helps PBS to create a supportive and structured environment for students' well-being.

The formalisation of PBS took place in the 1980s in the United States as a response to the growing need for effective behavioural management strategies in educational institutions. Reports showed how the traditional disciplinary system heavily relied on punishments and tough calls like suspension and with the emergence of PBS these punitive measures were replaced by systematic interventions to foster a positive and supportive learning environment. The foundation of PBS rests on three tiers of support: universal interventions for all students, targeted interventions for at-risk students, and intensive interventions for individual students with significant challenges.

Tier-1: Universal Intervention: under this tier the schools were to adopt a common set of behavioural expectations such as the values of respect, responsibility and safety and these were communicated to the students through mediums like posters, engaging lectures, discussions, and so on. This way the PBS was promoted to a majority of students.

Tier-2: Targeted Intervention: this include small group programmes focusing on specific social skills, mentoring or check-in/check-out system. These programmes were crafted out in such a way that the students were given more frequent feedback on their behaviour. This kind of intervention used a data driven approach to track and identify students who required a more structured support. These targeted interventions were effective in reducing disruptive behaviour and improving academic results for at-risk students.

Tier-3: Intensive Intervention: this is the most personalised support system and was designed for those with significant behavioural challenges. These interventions mainly involved the identification of any underlying cause of such challenges and according to that report the individualised behaviour intervention plans or BIPs were made. Methods under this intervention included one-on-one mentoring, therapeutic services and if required incorporating mental health professionals. This intervention tried to tailor strategies as per the need of a particular student with a particular behavioural challenge.

Very soon the adaptation of PBS went beyond the borders of the United States and garnered international attention and implementation in Canada, Australia and several European nations. These countries recognized the effectiveness of positive behaviour and included it as an integrated part of their educational system. The most noteworthy moment in the journey of PBS happened when in 1990s researchers and practitioners recognized the effectiveness of the PBS and began to collaborate across borders by sharing insights, practices and empirical research. This collaboration helped in tailoring its application to cultural contexts to show its effectiveness in diverse educational settings.

Organisations such as the Association for Positive Behaviour Support (APBS) played a crucial role in bringing together educators, researchers and policymakers from around the world and hosted annual conferences to discuss innovative strategies, research findings and case studies in order to promote and implement PBS. This endeavour helped in fostering a spirit of collaboration that transcended the geographical boundaries. These kinds of establishments proved beneficial not only for the students but also for the educators as they were now being equipped with necessary skills and knowledge in forms of training materials, workshops. These initiatives also helped in customization of the policies as per the local needs such as cultural and educational practices.

Australia embraced PBS as a part of their inclusive education system. PBS gained huge momentum as new initiatives were starting to take shape in Australia such as "School Wide Positive Behaviour Support" which was adapted to implement PBS to fit the Australian educational context. Alongside the school environment it ensured community involvement as well. Similarly Canada and other European nations soon adapted the PBS. The Canadian provinces of British Columbia and Ontario developed provincial initiatives that aligned with PBS principles, promoting positive behaviour and mental health support in schools. Moreover various international organisations like UNESCO being one of them advocated the practice of inclusive education and emphasised on positive behaviour support. Similarly WHO also recognized the importance of mental health in the educational setting and PBS's principle of emotional well being of students were also taken under consideration.

On a global scale the implementation of the PBS was though successful and was not without any challenges. Variability of training, resource and cultural perception often became obstacles in the smooth implementation. Yet PBS had and has been gaining traction throughout the world for its proven record of fostering holistic development of students.

The Indian educational framework on the other hand has been facing several challenges throughout the years post independence. Sometimes its academic pressure, disruptive behaviour of peers, and social and economic disparities. Thus In a country like India PBS becomes the most needed framework for several structural reasons.

To Address behavioural issues: Indian classrooms have a record of prevalent cases of disruption and bullying. According to the record of the National Commission for Protection of Child Rights, a significant percentage of children in Indian schools from various parts of the country experience bullying on regular terms which not only hampers their studies but also initiates a scar on their mental health. While traditional measures like suspension and expulsion are not always proven to be effective in these cases, PBS is an effective way of mitigating such behaviours with its proactive approach of monitoring and reinforcing these disruptive behaviours. Indian schools which have so far implemented PBS have reported to see a significant change in such disciplinary incidents.

To promote Social-Emotional Learning: a report of the World Bank shows how the number of Indian students with mental health issues are gradually rising with each year. A large percentage of students are seen to have clinical issues of anxiety, depression and rage. In such a state the social emotional learning (SEL) as a part of the academic curriculum becomes of utmost importance that would guide the children to navigate through the complexities of their educational and personal lives. In order to implement SEL, first the schools are needed to implement PBS which explicitly teaches skills like respect, empathy, self-regulation and resolution. It is proven that those schools in India which have implemented PBS have seen a great change in the students who now have learned the art of emotional resilience.

To Enhance Academic Performance: A study in the Journal Of Educational Psychology shows that schools which have utilised PBS experienced improvements in the students grades and classroom engagement levels. Positive behaviour directly influences the learning of a student. Reports show that in India the schools with PBS in their curriculum have seen notable increase in the academic performance of the students with a drastic decrease in absenteeism. With a lesser amount of disruptive behaviours students can engage more meaningfully in their education.

To Support Diverse Needs: an Indian classroom is anything but homogenous. Students come from different social, economical and cultural backgrounds. PBS with its mindfully tailored interventions meets the unique needs of the students, allowing them to have a personalised support system that would fit their individual needs. PBS with its targeted interventions makes sure that no student is left behind and this way brings an overall development. For example the National Education Policy (NEP), 2020 emphasises on the inclusive education which aligns with the prospects of PBS. Hereby schools are given the authority to implement tiered interventions for students requiring additional assistance. Another example can be the Pratham Education Foundation that utilises the PBS's interventions to support students from the marginalised sections of the country.

The Indian education system in the modern times has tried to implement a more learner friendly approach but yet there is a long way to go and for that the implementation of PBS in the Indian education system becomes vital. In the early ages the emphasis was always given on the characteristic development of a child who would go to the Masters or Gurus but in recent times knowledge has become a little limited to books and curriculum which can be altered with an effective use of the positive behaviour system.

Chapter-2: Role of Culture and Values in Shaping Behaviour

If Indian culture is a rich fabric of tradition then the wisdom of the ancient scriptures are the vibrant thread that weaves the patterns of values. Positive Behaviour System also takes its honourable place in that tapestry. The virtues brought in by the PBS such as kindness, empathy, responsibility, respect culminates to give birth to the virtue of Righteousness as a pivotal point of Indian thought. Each of these lessons of the ancient Indian scripture are imbibed with the knowledge of collective consciousness, harmonious relations. If looked closely we can see how till to this day the compassionate acts are the strength of the Indian community and these positive actions are the results of the Positive Behaviour traits as discussed in the scriptures which has been bearing the legacy of ethical conducts for the preceding generations. The Vedas, Upanishads and the epics like Mahabharat and Ramayana form the framework of what we now call PBS through their discussion of the virtues like truthfulness, non-violence, compassion, and self discipline. In Bhagavad Gita, a conversation between Lord Krishna and Arjun brings forth the entirety of Indian philosophy on positive behavioural traits through the advice of Lord Krishna wherein he dictates the whole human race through Arjun to act in accordance with righteousness, keeping in mind the moral duties. In Gita Krishna advocates Arjun to follow the path of purity which aligns with the modern idea of PBS where individuals are asked to act from a place of goodwill rather than ignorance and impulse. When looking at PBS through the lens of Ancient scriptures we can see how it provokes individuals to foster an environment that would reward constructive behaviours and provides advice on how to rise above narrow selfish ideas and cultivate a cultural positivity.

In almost all Indian scripture we can see how the PBS has been implied by moral fables to show the consequences of positive and negative behaviours. The revered characters also hold a vital role in embodying these traits and become personifications of such virtues. Such as the tales of Rama, laxman, and Hanuman from Ramayana and Yudhishthir from Mahabharata became the moral beacons of righteousness, devotion and truthfulness encouraging the readers and the devotees to follow theses traits of positive behaviour in their lives as well. The age-old scriptures, written by our ancestors, are their gifts to the coming generations to whom the PBS will be reinforced at the time of need by teaching them the benefits of positive behaviour as opposed to the negative ones.

PBS also serves as the centre point of Indian communal practices. In the ancient scriptures PBS is termed also as selflessness where every individual thinks not only about their own well-being but that of the whole community at large. There is no place for shallow selfish thoughts neither in the scriptures nor in the idea of PBS. The ethos that are the pillars of our ancient scriptures, has the idea of 'Seva' or selfless service at its heart. In every community during any festivity its common to see the values of being inclusive and having a broad mindset which is that Indian festivities are more or less celebrated as a community and seldom as individuals. The idea of positive behaviour as documented in the scripture shows how selflessness not only nourishes the body but sows the seeds of deep connection that blooms as a sense of compassion and unity. The Indian community has been standing on this value of PBS where one must elevate the entire community with themselves ever since and thus in the study of PBS we must not forget the wisdom of ages that has taken its shape through this scriptures.

Positive behaviour support (PBS) has roots in Indian culture, ancient scriptures, and mythology, where promoting values like compassion, non-violence, respect, and righteousness has been central. Here are some examples from ancient Indian books, mythology, and Vedic literature:

Ahimsa: Ahimsa means non-violence and it is one of the many aspects of PBS. In the sacred verse of Bhagavad Gita, Lord Krishna advocates the virtue of non-violence to Arjuna. In his words Ahimsa is not only an absence of harm but it transcends mere physical harm and extends to the values of compassion in thoughts also. This piece of advice that Krishna imparts to Arjuna who was about to set foot for the battle of Kurukshetra against his brothers is a timeless tenet which echoes through Buddhism and Jainism as well. Non-violence is a way to redemption from the shackles of narrow-minded beliefs and this is the same requirement as to be found in the idea of PBS where it becomes a means to achieve harmonious relationships, empathetic nature, and moral guidance.

Seva: Seva is the virtue of compassion and it is embodied by Lord Rama in the Epic Ramayana. According to the epic Seva is not only a virtue to practise towards one's community but also towards one's enemies. In Ramayana Lord Rama cremates his greatest enemy Ravana with proper honour and rites and this becomes a timeless example of compassion. This act of Lord Rama reflects how empathy must transcend rivalry and the dignity of an individual lies in their treatment of their enemies. Within PBS, this value inspires a culture of respect and service and fosters an environment where empathy thrives. The scripture teaches how services towards others must not be regulated by expectations. Under the terms of PBS, too we can see how kindness and mutual respect can only transform a society for the better.

Vidura Neeti: Vidura is a character of the epic Mahabharata and he is the beacon of wisdom as he advises the king Dhritarashtra with his profound insights and and 'Vidura Neeti' or ethical conduct. Vidura Neeti consists of the teachings of self-control, justice, and righteousness. He urged the king to embrace forgiveness over harshness. The Vidura Neeti serves as a moral compass that leads to the path of harmonious living. Under the lens of the PBS this wisdom of the vedic age becomes more relevant as it encourages individuals to make ethical choices to build a community of integrity.

Yajnas: in the Rig Veda Yajna is a sacred practice of sacrifice and not mere religious ceremonies. It was an expression of collective well-being. Individuals came together for such sacred sacrifices with shared purpose, reinforcing bonds of cooperation and responsibility. Within the PBS this principle inspires to engage in communal activities and celebrate the collective effort and mutual support.

Satyagraha: in the teachings of Upanishad the term Satya or truth emerges and from satya takes form the virtue of Satyagraha or adherence to truth. This ethical conduct is a guide towards authenticity of thoughts and deeds. Satyagraha creates an atmosphere of trust and respect and when someone pledges to Satya in life, they bring in a reign of honesty and integrity. This reverberates through the values documented in PBS where individuals are welcomed to act with transparency and sincerity by prioritising truthfulness as the building block of a community.

Selfless Detachment: in Bhagavad Gita Lord Krishna advises Arjuna to continue his actions without thinking about the results of his labour. This advice of Krishna focuses on the value of good deeds and the spirit of service. He urges Arjuna to believe that by bringing good upon others he is bringing the same results on himself. Under PBS as well we see how emphasis has been given on collective wellbeing, creating a culture where compassion and dedication thrive. By doing this we create a supportive environment for everyone including ourselves.

Respect for All Beings(Inclusivity): Athrava Veda holds the doctrine of interconnectedness of life and advocates the welfare of not only humans but also animals and nature. The scripture gives the message and directs us to instil deep respect for all living entities. In Atharva Veda this idea of inclusivity gives the profound message of coming out of the narrow-centredness of the mind and feeling the same compassion and empathy for everyone irrespective of their kind. The PBS theory, too, holds this virtue at top as a way to create the nurturing environment for all to thrive where every voice is valued and all forms of beauty in life are cherished.

Not only the ancient scripts and the epics but also the characters from these epics become symbols of values like truthfulness and righteousness. As previously discussed the character of Lord Rama is the embodiment of righteousness and empathy who not only values his own dignity but also that of his enemy Ravana. Similarly we find another character in the Ramayana who embodies unwavering devotion and selfless service to Lord Rama to whom he had pledged his alliances. This exemplifies the virtue of integrity. He becomes a positive role model with his courage, humility and perseverance to inspire others to rise above fear. These traits in Hanumana are the earliest example of positive role model and leadership to guide others in the path of virtuous behaviour. On the other hand, Mahabharata offers the character of Yudhisthira, the eldest Pandava as a symbol of patience and forgiveness. Despite being wronged multiple times, he often chose the path of peace and reconciliation over conflict, emphasising moral duty over personal vendetta. He adheres to justice and moral clarity even at the greater personal cost and teaches that leadership is rooted in empathy and honesty. The character of Yudhishtira upholds the principles of PBS such as emotional regulation, conflict resolution and positive interaction through forgiveness and understanding.

The discussion of Positive Behaviour System would be incomplete without drawing in from the Rigveda which is considered as the ultimate origin of Indian culture and philosophy. In many verses of the Rigveda the ethos of harmony, self-discipline and mutual respect can be found. This sacred text weaves in the knowledge of ages and creates a tapestry of moral codes to guide individuals towards a healthy life and communal well-being. Through its teaching the text echoes the very essence of the PBS by celebrating collective welfare and harmonious relationships. This timeless text of precious wisdom advocates the significance of balanced life with the self as well as the community at large. Here are some verses that directly directs the mankind towards embracing an ethical life and aligns perfectly with the strategies of PBS:

1. Promotion of Self-Discipline and Dharma (Righteousness)

Verse Example: "संगच्छध्वं संवदध्वं सं वो मनांसि जानताम्" (Rigveda 10.191.2)

Translation: *"Move together, speak together, let your minds be in unison."*

This verse promotes unity, self-discipline, and harmony within a group or society, emphasizing cooperation. PBS in schools or communities often involves teaching individuals to work together positively, respecting rules and maintaining order.

2. Emphasis on Respect and Non-Harm

Verse Example: "अहिंसा परमो धर्मः" (Although the exact phrase is from later texts, the principle of non-violence can be traced to Rigveda.)

Translation: *"Non-violence is the highest duty."*

Respect for others and non-harm is a central element of positive behaviour in classrooms, workplaces, and family life. The Rigveda teaches that acting without violence and respecting others' rights fosters peace, which can be aligned with behaviour management strategies that encourage empathy and kindness.

3. Encouraging Knowledge and Wisdom Sharing

Verse Example: "आ नो भद्राः क्रतवो यन्तु विश्वतः" (Rigveda 1.89.1)

Translation: *"Let noble thoughts come to us from all directions."*

This verse encourages the sharing of knowledge and wisdom fosters a collaborative and respectful environment. In a PBS framework, this can be seen in strategies that promote positive reinforcement through shared learning and mutual respect for diverse ideas.

4. Fostering Community and Collective Well-Being

Verse Example: "इन्द्रं वर्धन्तो अमुरः कृणुध्वं पाजसा ससम्" (Rigveda 10.42.1)

Translation: *"By strengthening each other, may we prosper with shared vitality."*

This verse emphasises collective growth and mutual support, essential principles of PBS. It promotes the idea that encouraging positive behaviour helps not just individuals but strengthens the whole community.

5. Promoting Gratitude and Positive Reinforcement

Verse Example: "उत त्ये तत सुक्रतुं देवासो अक्रन्नुक्थाशसं मघवत्वं वसूनाम्" (Rigveda 1.37.1)

Translation: *"The gods have bestowed upon us all good things, let us offer gratitude and sing their praises."*

Positive reinforcement, through expressions of gratitude and recognition of good deeds, is an essential component of PBS. This practice is reflected in Rigveda, where gratitude for blessings and positive outcomes is regularly emphasised.

6. Encouraging Moral Responsibility and Ethical Leadership

Verse Example: "यथा पूर्वे अजयन्ता पुराजाः" (Rigveda 7.33.3)

Translation: *"Just as the earlier leaders, lead with righteousness."*

The emphasis on ethical leadership highlights the importance of role models in shaping behaviour. In a PBS setting, leaders or teachers are expected to set positive examples for others to follow.

In conclusion we can see that this idea of PBS is not something novel, it has been a part of a timeless wisdom that was given to mankind in the forms of epics like Mahabharata and Ramayana and scriptures like the Upanishad and Vedas. It is the legacy of the foresightedness of our forefathers who knew that this knowledge and guidance would always be significant to human development. They had weaved the tapestry of the ethics required for moral conduct and harmonious coexistence which we now know by the name Positive Behaviour System Support and by drawing on these virtues and teachings we will be able to create a bridge between the wisdom of the past and the actions of the present which will in turn create a bright and prosperous future.

Chapter-3 Understanding Indian School Culture and Context

The education system of any country stands like a testament of the nation's growing history and evolving philosophy and India is no exception. The trajectory of Indian education narrates the development of the culture of the country and the challenges and hurdles it overcame. The Indian education system has its roots in those austere gurukuls in the cradle of nature, away from the materials of life and hidden from any politics. In those Gurukuls young boys would take refuge under the guidance of the Guru for as long as it took them to be prepared to face the world with the wisdoms as their arsenal. We can say that those huts of the Gurus are the evolved classrooms that we have today. At the heart of these Gurukuls lies the foundation of Character Development. From those days when a child needed to leave the comforts and care of his family to spend the days of his life under the guidance of the Guru, values were instilled for character building alongside academic pursuits. Today's Positive Behaviour System that is being introduced in the modern classrooms are just a reflection of those ancient exercises and shows the constant quest to not only nurture the intellect but also broadening the ideas of resilience and integrity.

Ancient Wisdom:

As already discussed, the Indian ancient education system can be traced to the Vedic age when Gurukuls were the only way the male children could acquire knowledge from the wise gurus. Under the tutelage of the gurus these pupils were not just students but disciples who followed the words of their teacher and thrived in the environment of respect, discipline and moral development. The concept of textbook was still absent and the only source of knowledge was weaved by the narrations of the Gurus and they overflowed with the lessons that made the students ready for the world outside the Gurukul. The subjects discussed in Gurukuls were philosophy, mathematics and arts but that was not all. These subjects constituted only a part of their training but the main focus was to teach the budding youth the virtues of honesty, compassion and humility. In the vedic age worldly knowledge was pertinent but more than that emphasis was given to the importance of characters and education was seen as a media through which a righteous society could be created. The atmosphere of the Gurukuls was rather holistic where collective endeavour was given much priority than individual efforts which aimed at a spiritual growth. It was believed since then that the bond between a teacher and a student is a sacred one built on mutual respect and shared values. The education system of ancient India knew how the welfare of the society depends on the positive characteristics of its members.

As India entered the mediaeval era the gurukuls started to get a different form and name such as madrasas and pathshalas and the spectrums of the ancient gurukuls changed while the essence remained the same. These institutions now started to incorporate a more diverse range of subjects and philosophies but the elementary emphasis on ethical conduct remained intact. Alongside the subjects of Gurukuls now the education system was more expanded with the studies of logic, poetry and science. Nevertheless the age was not free of its limitations as at this age education was not accessed by all sections of the society. Inclusivity was absent and the challenge of ensuring that every student will be offered the same guidance to become responsible citizens persisted.

Enter to Modernity:

The British Colonial period was like a whirlwind in the evolution of the Indian education system when suddenly a lot of external forces imposed their methods and models into the age-old structure of education. Suddenly the character building was replaced by the method of creating compliant bureaucrats and the British model of teaching and the significant use of the English language forged its place. This examination drive western method of teaching overshadowed the ethical dimensions that had previously been central. Yet voices like Mahatma Gandhi and Rabindranath Tagore urged the countrymen to return to the former holistic approach where education was to cultivate moral responsibility. These thinkers became spokesperson to a kind of education system that would regulate the emotions such as empathy, awareness and still pave the way for academic success.

In the post independence era India once again had the chance to reshape the education system. The newly formed constitution enshrined education as a fundamental right with emphasis on inclusivity and empowerment. In the 21st century once again the positive behaviour support system emerged as a reshaped and powerful framework suitable for the present generations. With a structured and proactive approach PBS emphasised respect, responsibility and community engagement. It was in a way an old approach in a new light as the roots of such knowledge goes way back to the days of Gurukuls where character development was as pertinent for a young mind as the learning process.

Today the Indian education system stands at the crossroads of globalisation and ethnicity. Alongside the academic change of curriculum the integration of technology and innovative pedagogy has opened a new door to character development. The new shift in the system places the students outside the walls of the classroom and gives them a guided platform to practise critical thinking and face the real world issues. As India welcomed NEP in 2020 it ensured an environment of collaboration and engagement. Yet these innovations are heavily indebted to the past wisdom where education is not only about the intellect but also a process of shaping compassionate and responsible citizens. Today with all the possible means at hand the students are required to be more aware of the importance of the character over words and they need to maintain this delicate balance in order to create a platform of integrity and compassion for the future generations.

In recent years, the educational landscape in India has increasingly recognized the need for effective discipline strategies that align with the principles of Positive Behaviour Support (PBS). While some Indian schools have begun to implement these strategies, many still rely on traditional, punitive methods that can undermine student engagement and growth.

Existing discipline strategies in Indian schools:

While India has embraced the evolved education system in many ways in some parts of elementary education few limitations are still persisting.

Punitive Measures: Under the traditional approach many schools in India still take the help of punitive measures like suspension, detention and other corporal punishments in order to shape the characters of the students. But these punishments are not much reformative as they either instil fear in the child or make them more adamant. Instead of taking up the punishments as the quick reflex the authority must forge a system wherein the root cause of such behaviour can be clearly understood. Researches have shown how such drastic measures often sow the seeds of anxiety and depression in a child from an early age and that is the biggest hindrance to their ultimate development.

Authoritarian Approach: Rule and order is the basic requirement of an institution but it is equally important to know and think through the implementation of the rules. A strict authoritarian approach to students mostly creates a culture of fear rather than respect and collaboration. It is true that in a classroom a teacher is in charge but teachers must know that the students are not mere subjects but the primary unit of a classroom.

Inconsistent application: in many schools the behaviour system has yet not been taken seriously and thus for a particular behaviour the consequences differ with teachers. This leads to confusion among children and more concerningly sometimes children perceive the unfairness and they lose their faith in their mentors and the disciplinary system.

Inefficiency of Teachers: In many Indian schools even to this day the lack of efficient teachers is the most concerning hindrance in implementing effective discipline strategies. Without the proper training the teacher often takes resort in the outdated methods that do not align with PBS principles. This kind of reactive approach fails to address the complex behavioural issues and further complicates the solutions.

In this age, thus the effective discipline strategy for education has become a pressing issue as schools have started to acknowledge the significance of fostering positive behaviour and it has become essential to integrate PBS principles. Fortunately recently many Indian schools are taking up the PBS to tailor their needs and has seen a significant improvement in overall academic performances. For instance, in a government school in Delhi adopted a peer mediation program trained mediators facilitated conflict resolution among their peers. This initiative cultivated a culture of empathy within the school community. Yet there is a long way ahead and to cover that distance certain changes in the institutional strategies are more vital.

Indian schools need to shift from punitive measures to restorative practices. Instead of being reactive a more structured proactive approach is the need of the hour to maintain the fundamental shift in discipline philosophy. This approach will ensure accountability and will foster a focus in repairing relationships. By implementing peer mediation and restorative circles allow students to reflect on their behaviours and its impact on others. Before implementing the behavioural system it becomes essential to set a clear structured list of expectations. Schools must work on making a code of conduct and the possible consequences beforehand and these lists are needed to be communicated to the students, teachers and parents with clarity. This approach creates a sense of shared responsibility among students who realise that the behaviour decorum is not just another rule for them rather it is a collaborative effort of both their school and theirs. Schools must remember that they are dealing with children and teenagers and they need to be motivated to perform the expected virtues and reinforcing their effort is the best way to keep them motivated to follow the code of conduct. By arranging some reward system such as 'merit points' or a recognition can make them see how their good conducts are being celebrated and they would feel the urge to follow the desired behaviour. A private school in Bengaluru established a positive reinforcement system where students earn 'kindness points' for acts of good behaviour. These points can be redeemed for rewards, fostering a culture of appreciation and motivation. This initiative not only reduced disciplinary incidents but also strengthened relationships among students and staff. This will not contribute to a positive school environment but also significantly reduce disciplinary incidents.

In India to create a PBS-aligned discipline strategy comprehensive training programs for teachers are essential. Preparing teachers for the PBS system workshops is the best way to help them acquire the skills of classroom management, conflict resolution and effective communication. These skills will empower the teachers with the necessary resources necessary to foster a climate of positive behaviour in the classroom and promote a culture of learning and adaptation. Moreover parents and the community must be involved in the learning process of the students. By regular communication with the parents reporting them the progress of the child's behaviour can also make them aware of the behavioural expectations of the school. In this way PBS will not remain within the walls of the schools and parents can, too, take a stand in maintaining the conduct at home.

However the implementation of PBS in India has many dimensions to it. The name of the country carries a rich history of culture and a diverse range of socio-economic backgrounds. The society of India is almost a living breathing entity which has a power to change and regulate everything within its territory and education is no exception. The education system is pivoted upon the social aspect of life and therefore society has its direct effect upon the evolutions it has gone through. Since the beginning of civilization the Indian society has been stratified under the stratas of economic disparities, accessibility of education and other segments. Students from an affluent background have always been able to access better educational facilities while students with lower socio economic backgrounds may only get the chance of accessing under-resourced schools. Under such social structure and economic imbalance it becomes difficult to extend the knowledge of PBS equally to every child. While well off students accessed the system quite smoothly the rest cannot. In the low-resourced schools they remain subjected to the traditional methods which unfortunately undermines the values of PBS. The disparity grows even further as these economically deprived students fail to get the parental and peer support and most of the time they fight the adverse and unpleasant aspects of their conditions which contaminates and wrongly influences their behaviour.

India being an arena of mixed cultures has an immense cultural and community influence placed on the education system and institutions. The ideas and values of each community differ from the other and this creates a lapse in the smooth flow of such an effort. Teachers and institutions who are implementing the PBS need to be constantly aware and mindful about the sensitivity of cultural differences and communal nuances to build a relationship of trust with the diverse group of students.

Chapter-4: Core Principles of Positive Behaviour Support

PBS is a framework but more than that it is a thought that can bring an immense amount of change in the society by moulding and directing the young minds. PBS makes one realize the inner potentials irrespective of the surroundings. In ancient days the Gurus took their disciples into the depth of the forests where all amenities of life were absent and in that bare minimum state they were bestowed with the knowledge of the inner wealth that is even more precious than the diamonds and rubies; that is the rich characters that they often grew into. PBS resonates with the wisdom that makes the individual to be aware of the inner lotus which like the actual flower grows with all its beauty and purity even in the murkier waters. It gives a blueprint to nurture emotional strength and intelligence within the educational systems and when positive behaviour is celebrated and reinforced a school can be transformed into a thriving community of mutual respect. To understand how PBS works in fostering the inner wealth it is important to delve into the core principles of PBS which gives a clear cognition of the significance of PBS in young minds.

Promoting Emotional Intelligence and Empathy in Positive Behavior Support:

This principle of PBS is vital for fostering a supportive school environment. emotional intelligence is the ability to recognize, understand, and manage one's own emotions and those of others. This is an important aspect of understanding the way the children are interacting with each other, resolve conflicts and build relationships. For example if a school decides to incorporate a fun learning system under PBS framework where every student are asked to take turn to act out the various emotions without using words while the peers will be on the receiving end, this exercise will be proved to be helpful in helping student not only to be aware but to cultivate different emotions. This kind of exercise teaches children the impact of such emotions on others. So in class with students of different temperament if such an activity is introduced it can be seen that a child who usually reacts defensively when criticised and struggles to understand the feelings of his fellow classmates, will slowly recognize the subtle cues and understand that his behaviour might have caused some unpleasant feelings in his peers. This kind of practical application of emotional intelligence in the classroom helps the student to navigate their feelings and create an atmosphere of empathy. In the age of social media where human connection is at stake and the worst impact of this technological development is falling on the children who often fail to absorb the good and leave the harmful effects. Thus a face to face interaction to understand the nuances of human interaction becomes extremely crucial for this generation. This kind of practical approach prepares students for life beyond schools. In the long run these lessons are beneficial for their personal and professional life. As adults the ones with this knowledge become more resilient, adaptable and capable of leading with compassion.

Building Respectful Student-Teacher Relationships in Positive Behavior Support:

The most elementary aspect of the PBS is the teacher-student relationship that works like a foundation of PBS. Such a relationship is needed in order to create an environment of trust and mutual respect. It is the duty of a teacher to make a student feel safe and valued in the classroom to engage them in education and positive activities. It's of utmost importance that a teacher should take notice of his pupils temperament and engagement and not just the syllabus. If they notice a decline in the engagement of students in class it is a sign that something is bothering them or they are losing interest in academic learning. In such a condition the teacher must resolve to some innovative strategies that would first make the students attentive to his class and his lectures before he continues any further with the syllabus. In such a case the teacher can arrange a session in the class where the students will not be taught but will be asked to participate in an interaction wherein they will share their interests, aspirations and challenges in a space which is free of any judgments. If the teacher shows his unfaltering attention to them and listens to them mindfully it will give an impression to the students that they are taken seriously by the authoritative figure and might reflect the same respect to the teacher as well. constructive conversation has myriad positive effects upon the students and creates a bond between the teacher and the students- not only making them attentive in the class but also to win the confidence of the students which fosters a classroom of respect, kindness and mutual support. Furthermore such a bond between a student and their teacher helps the child to confine to the teacher with some issues he might have been facing outside the school. Before teaching the syllabus and guiding the students towards academic excellence it is pertinent for the teacher to help the students to feel safe and valued inside the class. This foundational principle is vital as it creates a positive impression on the children's mind about mutual respect which in their adult years help them to navigate their difficulties.

Encouraging Peer Support and Positive Peer Influence in Positive Behavior Support:

Peer support in a school environment helps to build positive behaviour. Positive peer influence often proves to be the best way out of a situation where the involvement of teachers is not that effective. The guidance and support that can be given to a struggling student by their peers fosters a sense of validation and a culture of support and unity among the students. It is the responsibility of the school to create a system where students can participate to support and seek support from their peers freely. For example when a new student joins the school it becomes extremely hard for them to accommodate with the school rules and more than that to find a place among their peers. The new students are always subjected to varied feelings of intimidation, fear and alienation. But if the school offers a special program where every new student will be grouped with one or a group of old and elder students who will be incharge of making the new child at ease by navigating that student through the intricacies of the school life and helping them to settle. In most of such cases it has been seen how such activity helped the new student not only to accommodate faster but also become more engaged in class activities. Moreover with such an approach the rough years of adolescence can be directed for the better. With a supportive environment to thrive the children would steer away from the negative aspect of it and would learn the positive attributes that he himself has received from his peers. Peer support creates a more inclusive and ragging free environment where gradually a sense of unity fosters among students. By enforcing peer support under the framework of PBS we can pave the way for a more empathetic generation.

Incorporating Mindfulness and Stress Management in a Positive Behaviour System:

In the 21st century stress has become an unwanted companion to humankind. Irrespective of age stress has affected every single person. Especially the children who suffer from it without a clear idea how to control and manage it. The academic life has made the schedule of the students in India hectic and on top of that they are often burdened to excel in the extracurricular activities as well. parents and peers are pushing them in the rat race and this is creating an adverse effect on them. Under such circumstances the framework of PBS offers mindful activities and stress management in schools which has been proved to be a successful venture in the USA and European academic structure. Such a gesture from the school allows the students to focus well on studies by supporting them and letting them feel relaxed. The schools can arrange mindful sessions for students but in doing so they should structure it as per the needs of the students and not just make it a mundane part of the school routine. For instance right before any examination or semester students tend to go into a phase of extreme stress. This is the time for the authority to introduce a session or sessions of meditation for the students. These kinds of sessions will help them in releasing stress by practising breathing techniques and will also make them aware of their thoughts and worries to release the tension. After such a session the students will definitely feel the calm inside them and will be rejuvenated to prepare for their exams. This is an effective measure for the students who are showing disruptive behaviour due to some social pressure. The school can include a workshop in such a case, where the students will be allowed to share their experiences and learn to manage their emotions effectively by the techniques of deep breathing and journaling. Stress management and mindfulness help students to cope with pressure and that makes them resilient. By incorporating such methods the school creates a positive school climate where students will be equipped to handle their stress because without the personal growth of a child academic growth is also impossible to take place.

Individualization and Inclusion in a Positive Behaviour System:

A school must always remember that it is similar to a micro cosmos. Just like our society, the school is not a homogenous organisation. The school should and must recognize that each student is different in their strengths and their weaknesses and therefore each of them requires and deserves the unfaltering attention. By tailoring a curriculum that would meet the needs of every student the school fosters in the students the sense of being valued and supported that enhances their academic performances as well as their mindset.

If in a class one child struggles with reading then its expected of the school to implement a reading intervention to suit his need. If the school collaborates with professionals and seeks out a personalised learning plan for that student the issue might get cured once and for all. A child with any difficulty will have the tendency to restrict himself within a boundary of embarrassment and in such a time one-to-one tutoring sessions can improve his state as well as make him slowly become comfortable around strangers. This step helps a student with any difficulty to eventually gain confidence and resume the usual classes. In another scenario a collaborative classroom can foster a sense of community in the students by encouraging a teaching plan that will incorporate group studies, hands-on experiment and discussions. This way the students can build a sense of unity and empathy for each other and in need can help their fellow classmates in need. Inclusivity in a learning space builds a sense of belonging among the students and they feel valued and encouraged to share their limitations and interests more freely. Moreover by providing individualization and inclusivity the school can contribute to a more equitable education system. As under the PBS framework the students are given appropriate and personal care and attention that not only supports the dynamic structure of the classrooms but also bridges academic gaps.

Promoting Prevention Over Reaction in a Positive Behaviour System:

There has been a common belief that when one needs to kill an unwanted weed it is not wise to just chop the stemm, to completely finish it one needs to uproot the plant or better, to nip it in the bud. Likewise under PBS framework it is advised to be proactive when addressing a potential issue before it can escalate. Prevention is always the first priority and definitely better than cure. This strategy helps in building a positive school climate where students feel safe and supported and will not allow any disruptive behaviour pattern to take shape. A very contemporary issue is that of bullying and ragging in schools. Many schools used to wait for any incident of that kind to occur before they implemented any strict reaction. But recently it's coming to notice how schools are willingly following the PBS advice and implementing the anti-bullying program beforehand. Under this program the young children are being taught about the adverse side of the bullying on both the victim and the oppressor and alongside they are understanding the values of empathy, conflict resolution and effective communication. Sometimes it's seen how some students would;d miss certain classes which eventually affects their academic progress. In such cases the school can refrain from any reactionary measures like punishment or detention and address the underlying cause by simply arranging a private meeting with the alleged student and try to understand the reason for such action. In this way the student will feel more supported and valued and the attendance issue might be solved effectively.

In conclusion we can say that from the core objectives of PBS it is clear that a revolution can be brought in the society without any propaganda. No result comes out from instilling fear in students but greater goals can be set by implementing wise actions and consistently following them. All these principles of PBS were made for the well-being of the children who one day will be becoming citizens of the state and the process of making them able and virtuous starts from the elementary level of schools.

Chapter-5: PBS and Family Engagement

The central mission of a positive behaviour system is to create an environment for students where they can thrive academically as well as socially and emotionally. Therefore in PBS it is of paramount importance to design a framework to encourage and reinforce desirable behaviours in students. However the school walls are not the limitations of PBS as it extends beyond the boundaries of school and reaches the homes. In the very framework of PBS, family plays a crucial role as it amplifies the efforts taken by the school in reinforcing positive behaviour. PBS is like a collaborative endeavour of both school and families to support the student's growth. Furthermore it falls on the family of the students to make sure that they understand the expectations and find them more relatable. This chapter will focus on exploring the pivotal role that family engagements play in creating a holistic space for the student to thrive and learn. In the discussion of PBS it is crucial to delve deep into the strategies that can be implemented in order to cultivate trust among families, what practical tools are needed to involve families in the framework and most importantly to build a platform between the school and the family for effective communication.

Influences of Families and Parents:

According to Dr. Joyce Epstein, a renowned researcher in family engagement, said, "When schools, families and community groups come together to support learning, children tend to succeed not just in school, but throughout life." And this is precisely the crux of the whole idea. Researches have shown how family involvement in their children's education and learning can bring improvement and likewise their collaborative approach in implementing the PBS in the front of home has resulted in significant change in the behaviours of a child. The aim of PBS is to foster desirable behaviour by identifying and eliminating the negative ones. Therefore it is of utmost importance for the parents and the families to know and understand the clearly laid out expectations of PBS and try to reinforce them at home by merging them with the daily routines. In a study published in the Journal of School Psychology it was stated that the students whose parents and family actively engage themselves in the behaviour management strategies are less susceptible in showing traits of disruptive behaviour. If this alignment takes place between the school and the child's family it creates a strong harmony between the home and the school and the child easily internalises the positive behaviours.

Moreover family engagement in behaviour programs can foster a sense of belonging among students. They find a point of connectedness with their school and feel a sense of belonging in the school community. This sense of connection becomes even more vital for those students who are marginalised and need the inspiration to adapt the behavioural changes that they are being offered. With their families also involved in their learning , they feel secure and supported and more willingly adapt the behavioural suggestions that are offered to them.

Partnering with Families in Behaviour Support Plans:

It is true that the positive behaviour system can bring a subtle yet powerful change in the lives of students but at the same time the success of the framework is heavily hinged on the active and willing involvement of students' families. Schools can set expectations and guidelines but in order to make the plans more impactful the willing cooperation of the families are indeed vital. This partnership helps in the understanding of the goals of PBS and also in promoting a cohesive approach to the behaviour management. According to Dr. Anne T. D'Agostino, researcher in School Psychology, " involving families in the creation of the behaviour support plans not only enhances the plan's effectiveness but also builds trust and communication between schools and families." To elaborate on this statement it can be thought that by promoting a collaborative approach to the framework the school can make the families a critiquing figure in the whole process who will ensure not only the strategies but also will make sure that they are culturally relevant and tailored to the individual needs of the students.

While implementing a framework such as PBS it has to be kept in mind that the subjects are children and they are special in their own ways and these kids are in a vulnerable stage when they need to be handled with care and patience. Sometimes children feel shy and petrified in the school which hinders their progress and in such cases to deal with them better the school must gather some insight into the child's nature from their parents before takib\ng any action. Families can also provide a detailed context and idea to educators which is impossible for them to know of within the school. It is true that one can not do an experiment unless or until one understands the unit. Although the PBS is not any experiment yet it is a new path to tread on and in this case a detailed survey beforehand is required for achieving the desired result. Thus the Journal of Positive Behaviour Intervention says, " Parents' knowledge of their child's behaviour in various contexts can inform the development of more effective support strategies." This information becomes vital when the schools are needed to craft out a personalised approach for an individual student. But this engagement of family extends beyond an individual student. A collaborative climate of learning can influence the overall school. When a school values and fosters family involvement that sense of involvement resonates throughout the school community.

Culturally Responsive Approach to Parental Involvement:

Within the PBS framework, a culturally responsive approach towards families and a partnership with them enhances student's behaviour and engagement. Researches have shown how a school that respects and adapts a more culturally open approach has seen significant improvement in student's growth and have strengthened the school-home connection. According to Dr. Gloria Ladson-Billings, " Teaching requires an understanding of the cultural context of students and their families." This understanding must be taken seriously by the educators as the reinforcement of the PBS heavily indebted to the involvement of home. To build trust with the students the school and the educators should recognize the cultural norms while making the rules, guidelines and disciplines. Schools must understand that different families have different ways of collaborating with the school and thus it must always be kept in mind while hosting any program with the parents and the families, that the parents must feel comfortable and can put that trust in the school's system.

For this understanding of the cultural dynamics the educators need to be trained properly so that they can be equipped with the skills to understand and engage with diverse families meaningfully. Even the National Education Association has emphasised that training in cultural responsiveness is essential for educators to develop positive relationships with diverse families. A training program must be organised where teachers will be able to equip themselves with cultural norms, implicit biases and effective communication strategies. To make the students feel valued and supported, first it is crucial to make sure that they feel that the school or the organisation values and acknowledges their background as well. Cultural responsiveness of the school is not limited to the well equipped teachers; it is applicable to the very curriculum that the school follows which must be free from any stringent approach and will be an open space that welcomes changes and alterations as per requirement. What a child learns on a day to day basis has a massive impact on how they behave and how their family might think about the education that they are receiving. Therefore schools must embrace a culturally responsive curriculum that will acknowledge the cultural background of students. This process, as stated by multicultural education expert, Dr. Geneva Gay, will increase the students' engagement and motivation. In a Havard research process it has been discussed that;, " Community partnership can bridge the gap between schools and families, leading to increased parental involvement." In a country like India schools' partnership with the local organisations are immensely helpful as it allows the schools to provide help and support tailored to the needs of the underprivileged families and eventually will win their trust on the education of their child and this sometimes massively helps in the child's positive behavioural changes.

Conducting Parent Workshops and Training:

Parents' empowerment through workshops is crucial as it enables them to play a pivotal role in the child's behaviour. The school can teach and reinforce the strategies of PBS but the constant development of a child's behaviour takes place in their home among their family members and therefore it is important to arrange something in order to guide the parents in order to reinforce the positive behaviour strategies effectively to their children. Workshops are the best medium of developing not only a partnership between the school and the parents but also a platform where the parents can know the proper way of reinforcing the PBS. These workshops can cover a range of topics and strategies like positive reinforcement strategies, effective communication techniques and ways to identify and address challenging and disruptive behaviours in their children. These behaviour management programmes not only helps the schools to work in collaboration for a proper implementation of the PBS but also helps the parents to manage their child's behaviour on a domestic font, enabling them to engage in meaningful dialogues with their children about expectations and emotions. When the parents are guided to address the disruptive behaviours of their children through evidence-based strategies the parents become more equipped in addressing these issues more proactively rather than reactively.

These workshops need to be both interactive and culturally responsive. An interactive format of any workshop allows the parents to feel a sense of liberty in expressing their thoughts and also open-mindedly participating in hands-on experiences and discussions. The parents must be made to feel a sense of ownership in their children's development and for that educators should give them the opportunity to share their own strategies and stories, creating a community where families and parents will feel valued and connected. Other than the ideological factors of conducting workshops, schools should also take care of the logistical factors such as the timing of the workshops, keeping in mind the schedule of the parents and other resources such as flexibility of language preference. It is always recommended to use the vernacular language or the native tongue to offer clarity to such programs. As more parents will feel free to join these workshops the more benefited the children will be.

Communication Strategies between Teachers and Parents:

To ensure that both the school and the parents are aligned in their effort to bring the positive change in the student's behaviour, effective communication is of utmost importance. If a students' misbehaviour or challenging behavioural traits are important to be reported to the family then there must be regular communication between the school and the family. And experts have recommended the multiple communication channels as the best way to foster a connection between the two. These multiple channels can be emails and messages regarding the updates on the students' behaviour and performance or any school programme on the same. Other than that, personal phone calls for special cases can build a relationship with the parents and they will feel involved with the process of their children's growth. Not only to report any negative outcome but also to give the family updates on their children's progress is another vital aspect of this kind of communication. Schools can arrange meetings with parents more frequently and by not only limiting that to a general discussion they can focus specifically on behaviours and conduct. To make sure that parents actively participate on such meetings and conferences, more innovative change must be brought in the approach. These meetings can be a platform where parents can share the other contexts of their children and discuss their personal achievements or their nature in general which will help the school to conduct a more focused strategy for the students. In such meetings teachers often share their feedback and if this constructive feedback can be regularised and made more frequent then the parents will be able to reinforce the feedback more effectively. By implementing an effective communication between school and parents the agendas become clearer and help ultimately in building a relationship of trust and support. In this way teachers and parents become co-navigators in the child's journey towards growth and progress.

So in conclusion we can recall the famous proverb "Charity begins at home." The success of PBS depends not only on the efficacy of the school's PBS strategies but also how well those ideas are being communicated to the parents. If the school successfully makes the family involved and interested in this system then the path to desired outcome becomes more accessible. Thus in the process of bringing a positive change in not only the children but their families and culture,too, must feel valued and acknowledged.

Chapter-6: A Positive School-wide Positive Behaviour Support Framework

To foster a more inclusive and productive learning scenario schools must work on the essential framework that would help in the implementation of the PBS agendas. As the schools are striving to strike a balance in their curriculum and to incorporate not just academic experimentations but also bring a holistic change in the students' overall growth, they must realize and organize a structured way to approach it. A school-wide framework of PBS can fix the issues of any confusion in future regarding the expectations that the school wants to actualize in the coming future. As any architectural construction requires a blueprint before beginning their work of erecting the building in real life, likewise schools must take advantage of this framework to pin their expectations, goals, strategies and actions-hypothetical consequences. This framework does not work like a balance sheet but has more aspects to it as it is a way to proactively identify and acknowledge the diverse socio-economic and cultural background of the students and fashion the framework in such a manner as to value the dynamic structure through their agendas.

For building this structural approach to PBS there are a bunch of key components that the schools must keep in mind. Especially under the education system of India these components are much more pertinent to be adhered by.

1. The schools must acknowledge the diverse backgrounds of each student. The social economic and cultural dynamics are

not homogeneous in the school setting and require great attention to details when deciding upon a framework for the behavioral development of a child. Inclusivity being the elementary principle of PBS, must reflect through the framework as well where behavioral expectations should resonate with the cultural sentiment of the students and their families. It becomes the responsibility of the school to articulate the specific behavior goals ensuring that the students and their families understand and endorse them.

2. The curriculum needs to be structured and restructured according to the requirements to teach positive Behaviour alongside the academic courses. Social emotional learning must be incorporated in the curriculum with the help of fun activities such as interactive sessions, group projects and role-playing . This approach will promote empathy and cooperation in students.

3. In the Indian education system recognition is a vital medium of instruction and motivation. Not only academic performances but value should be given to any act of demonstrating positive behavior through praises and rewards. This can work as an encouragement for the positive traits they have practiced and would continue to motivate them throughout their life.

4. PBS framework should not exclude the involvement of parents as according to experts the involvement of parents and family helps in building the moral of the student and they feel supported. Moreover in the rural areas sometimes by engaging the parents helps in spreading a positive message to the families about the education of their children. Through workshops and discussions if the parents can be

made to realize the importance of such curriculum they can help the school greatly in the progress of the strategies.

5. The framework of PBS must be mindful of the different nature of students that they are dealing with and thus a tiered support system is mandatory. Alongside universal strategies schools must craft individualistic and targeted interventions for students who need that attention and care. Many students deal with a diverse range of issues- social awkwardness, emotional competencies are such issues that need some additional assistance.

6. Schools need to incorporate systems of tracking the behaviors of students both positive and negative which will allow the educators to identify any problematic area and foster appropriate interventions for that. Even for positive behavior, a data-driven approach helps in using those incidents as a source of encouragement.

7. Finally the most important component of the framework must be its flexible nature wherein it will openly adapt to any new change or feedback from students, educators and parents for better improvement and to maintain the effectiveness of the framework.

After the formation of the PBS framework the next step is to implement those agendas. The implementation of the PBS framework must be systematic and cohesive to ensure its effectiveness and sustainability. The process of implementation requires to follow certain steps such as establishing a leadership team, assessing the practices, defining the behavioral expectations, reinforcing, developing teaching strategies and regulating a monitoring system.

The expectations of the framework must be defined clearly keeping in mind the cultural relevance of the expectations. The expectations can only be regulated thoroughly when it is clearly communicated to all settings of the school. By guiding the educators to arrange a meeting with the guardians or parents, its schools' duty to put across the expected behavior goals to each individual in a cohesive manner. This can be next followed by a training program for the educators. As most of the time the idea of PBS gets lost among the teachers due to their lack of training, it is immensely pertinent to arrange a training for the teachers and educators wherein they will learn about PBS and the ways they can incorporate it in their teaching methods. Teachers must also be trained to identify the negative or disruptive or challenging behaviors in students and ways to handle them proactively rather than reactively. Once the teachers are trained then a teaching strategy must be formed where instructions will be given explicitly to use age-appropriate methods which are student-friendly and can create a bond of trust and respect between the teacher and the students. Since motivation is the key drive in any field of activity, students must feel valued and acknowledged for the positive behaviors that they would showcase. The reinforcement system can include verbal praises, rewards, certification and so on. This will encourage the students to retain the positive traits. Since PBS is a consistent effort, regular monitoring is of utmost importance inorder to retain the progress and to exceed it. Regular monitoring and review method can identify any disturbing behavior at an early stage. In such a case professional help can be included in the framework. Schools must arrange for parents-teacher meetings, workshops for parents and other interactive sessions with the guardians to send across the goal of PBS to them and to include the wider spectrum of family and community into the learning process. For the smooth implementation of the PBS framework in the school the involvement of the parents becomes crucial in fostering the emotional development and sense of support in the children beyond the school walls. There are no strict beginning or end of the Framework because the PBS structure calls for a flexible approach to instruction and implementation after following and communicating all the goals and expectations the schools must not draw a line. Since PBS prioritizes feedback the school must always prepare for change and alteration in their implementation method.

Role of School Leadership in Driving PBS:

To implement a sustainable Positive Behaviour Support System the schools need to have an able leadership. Leadership of a school is constituted of the Principal and the Administrators who play the pivotal role in the successful implementation of PBS in the school setting. At the initial stage it is responsibility of these Leaders to take charge of the cohesive establishment of the framework of the PBS by communicating the agendas and expectations to the educators and arranging a wide network to extend them to the communities. They are the ones who come up with a comprehensive and suitable framework for their respective school structure keeping in mind the consequences for infractions. By involving other stakeholders such as educators, professional experts, families of the students and also the communities they create a bond of ownership and accountability which promotes an appropriate conduct of the framework.

The school leaders are also responsible in training the educators to carry out the framework by equipping them with necessary skills and strategies like restorative practices, conflict resolution and so on. The empowerment of the teachers is the second most important criteria in the PBS framework and the duty of doing that lies with the able leaders of the school. The leadership of the school takes care of the professional growth of the teachers and educators which is as crucial as the growth of the students. The leaders are the ones who must take constant care for any chance to improve the framework. For example the administrative sector of the school carries out an evidence-based approach for their interventions and support system to specific needs through active monitoring. In addition to all the other strategies the most vital is that the school leadership must model the behaviors they wish to see in the students. The school leaders must demonstrate the same respect, empathy, and responsibility that they want to foster in the children with consistency. By setting a universal standard they can regulate the behavior that they want to extract from the children. Therefore the school leadership must focus on an overall growth of the institution and not just that of the children because a partial development of just the students will ultimately bear no result at all. So like a governing body the leaders must be inclusive to ensure the healthy climate of the school and a successful establishment of the PBS program.

Behaviour Matrix: Expectation and Rewards:

In the PBS framework the delineation of the expected behavior from students in various contexts is extremely crucial. In different contexts in the school like classrooms, playground, hall etc need to have a clear set of acceptable behaviors and corresponding rewards and the most comprehensive tool for such matters is a Behaviour Matrix. A Behaviour Matrix is a visual tool to guide the behaviors and the rewards and it also aligns with the school's value and mission. this Matrix has three core components: behaviors, expectations, and rewards.

In order to create a robust Behavioral Matrix the school first needs to identify the expected behaviors that aligns with the school's value system in embodying respect, safety and responsibility. Once the identification is done it is absolutely important to get them reviewed by the stakeholders – teachers, parents to make those expectations resonate with the community and to foster a sense of ownership and unity. In a classroom, values of respect, responsibility and safety are often observed through the behaviors of the students. For instance when they are in the classroom the students are expected to listen closely when others are speaking, they must follow the polite decorum and talk with a polite and humble diction and most important of all is to be open and receptive of diverse opinions. These behaviors will ensure the value of respect in the classroom. The next is responsibility and to imbibe the value in their behavior they must be made to complete their school work on time, be prepared for the class and should take full responsibility for their actions. Finally in a classroom students can create a safe environment by following the mandatory rules of the school, using the materials with care and maintaining the personal space. Thus to make these expectations coherent and memorable to the students the visual tool of the Behaviour Matrix can be used which will engage the students' interest with illustrations and tag lines to work like constant reminders to the students. If the educators can transform the classroom into a space of inspiration for the students the positive behaviors will gradually become an inseparable part of the curriculum.

Once the positive behaviors are identified the next crucial task is to motivate the student's enthusiasm and interest in applying these traits in their daily school life and the reinforcement comes from the reward systems that serves as a catalyst in nurturing the growth of the students positive behaviors. Schools can in this case structure a three tiered reward system that resonates with learners at different stages of development.

First tier: there can be immediate rewards through the verbal praising of the teachers to reinforce a small good gesture by a student. This small token of acknowledgement lifts the spirit of the children which keeps them interested to demonstrate more positive traits in the coming classes.

Second tier: The second tier can be short time rewards for students for those who have shown a demonstration of good behavior in class. This can be some special privileges of extra recess time or a small token to those who help others in need. These rewards will work as more than just mere tokens to the children and they will know that they are being valued and acknowledged by the ones in authority.

Third tier: Schools can arrange long term programs to honor and celebrate those who have displayed excellent behavior annually. This can include a small ceremonial certification event where the students with a record of consistent good manners will be rewarded in front of the whole school. These types of rewards not only pushes the particular student towards excellence but also motivates the rest to follow the same behavioral pattern in order to receive the same respect and honor from the school.

Once the expectations and rewards are established the next and last important task is to implement the Matrix systematically. For that the teachers can take a proactive role in incorporating the behavior matrix in the daily routine and using it as references in between lessons . like this with regular reinforcement and consistent practice students can be made aware of the importance of adapting these expectations.

In conclusion we can say that the PBS system and the framework is not just a simple guidebook that can be crafted by one person and can be implemented in a day within a blink of an eye. It is a varied, diverse and dynamic process that involves the whole school community's active participation. Every single person who is directly or indirectly associated with school is a stakeholder in this. The PBS framework and the Behaviour Matrix are the tools that help in building the community. If these two aspects of the PBS system is done with utmost attention and mindfulness and also under the close observation of the whole community then the task of fostering lifelong positive behaviors in students to guide them towards a brighter future will not be difficult at all.

Chapter-7: Positive Behaviour Support Strategies for Classrooms

PBS offers the best means to create a student friendly, healthy proactive classroom. Although we know that positive behavior can be exercised at home as well yet schools are majorly responsible for imbibing and reinforcing the positive traits in students and precisely it is the teachers who control and monitor the classrooms where the students spend the majority of their school hours. As the mentors of the students the teachers can use PBS as a form of communication with the students. As Jerome Schultz puts it "If you can read the need , you can meet the need" – the teachers can identify the behaviors by observing the communication of the student and that is why a healthy and safe classroom environment is much needed in PBS. To develop a positive classroom environment the teachers must build a relationship of trust with the children by communicating with them with empathy and compassionate curiosity. A healthy classroom can be formed if the teacher realizes and believes that all students are special and unique and they might need to ameliorate some behaviors in them but that too by understanding them and there is no need to fix them. Understanding the students demand a collaborative atmosphere where equal participation and fair chance of communication is provided. Often the students struggle to communicate or express due to some issues in their communication skills or they just feel intimidated or try to just avoid the tasks. There are times when a student behaves negatively which is a sign that the learning environment might not be helpful for them. As teachers these are the prompts that must be taken seriously and should be addressed immediately to formulate a response for it.

It has to be kept in mind that students can better meet the expectations when they know the clear set of expectations and thus in a school which has already taken up PBS classroom expectations should complement that model. Each expectation needs to be clearly defined and demonstrated to the students in an affirmative tone and not as orders or rebukes. In an effective classroom environment the expectations must be taught to the students by the teacher clearly and explicitly with examples and with involving the students, too, in the process of demonstration. Other than that the classroom design also becomes a powerful PBS strategy. The learning environment should not be rigid but flexible to support the activities like, small groups, group projects, collaborative discussion-based learning etc. by creating a free and bendable design of the classroom the fear and sense of intimidation can be solved from the students. Lastly a healthy classroom is incomplete without extending its traces beyond the school boundary. When families and communities will be involved in the process of learning the efforts of PBS will take one step towards success. Teachers must regularly communicate and keep the families informed of their child's progress and they should be frequently invited for workshops and meetings which will keep them equipped with the strategies to follow at home to support PBS. But even after all these PBS is initiated by the school and it takes shape in the classrooms only and therefore the beginning of the journey must be well structured and well constituted for the later progress.

Constructive Disciplining:

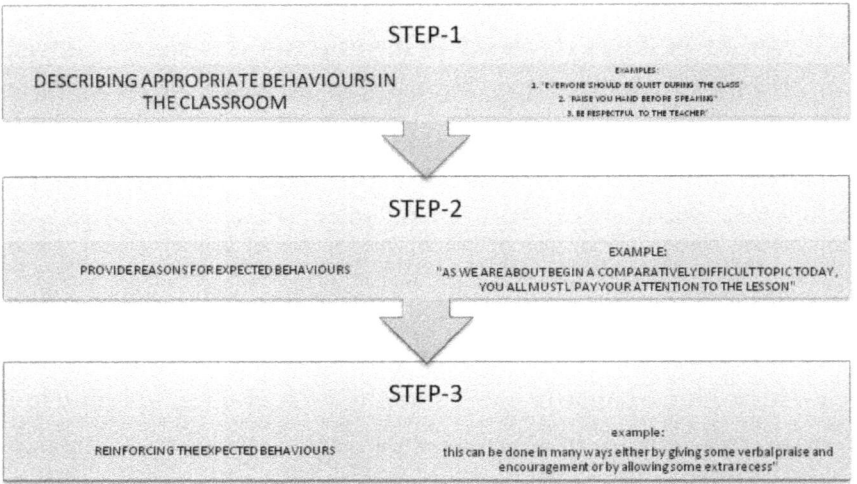

Role of Teachers in PBS:

In PBS teachers and educators are bestowed with the major challenge to work with the positive Behaviour strategies. Their role is not merely limited to the academic instructions but goes beyond the cultivation of a supportive and engaging classroom environment. The teachers in a class are the most vital part as they set the models of expected behaviors for the students to follow. Their actions alone can influence the student and bring a complete change in the atmosphere of the classroom. Here are a few methods that can be followed by the teachers in order to cultivate a supportive classroom environment.

Setting a model for the positive classroom behavior:

A study published in Educational Psychology shows how students are more likely to exhibit positive behaviors when they see their teachers practicing them. Respect and support is a shared value and in a classroom if the one in authority practices the values of respect and support then as a reflex the students tend to do the same. In a classroom students often observe the teacher, one in authority and if they see the teacher demonstrating respect, responsibility and support then it becomes a standard for the students to emulate. If the students see a teacher being empathetic and conversing with them in a polite manner and being respectful while addressing their mistakes, automatically the students will end up doing the same as they will learn that it is the correct conduct of a classroom.

Developing Classroom Routines:

Setting a clear routine for the classroom is extremely crucial. Before beginning a class the teachers must go through the tedious yet necessary process of setting a clear list of expectations that they want the students to follow. Not only that, this list must be communicated to the students in an explicit manner so that they don't feel confused or unsure of what is expected of them. For example the teacher can formulate certain hand signs for the students to indicate particular needs like raising hand when someone wants to communicate this way the students would learn to seek permission before putting forth their need. These expectations will allow the students to be consistent in their practice of PBS and will help the teacher in maintaining a supportive classroom environment.

Practicing Reinforcement:

According to Skinner 'Reinforcement is an overarching term for a continuously delivered consequence that is associated with an increase of future behavior'. As discussed earlier, consistent praises and attention is the most effective part of implementing PBS and this is often undertaken by the teachers. Teachers must observe, notice and note the behavioral changes in the students. Whensomeone shows immense improvement in their behavior or stays consistent in maintaining the expectations, the teacher must praise them with verbal praises or small tokens or acknowledgement. This works as a motivation in students. It does not always have to be a long term program where the students showing positive behavior would be awarded annually. In the small sphere of the classroom, on a daily basis these improvements can be noted and honored which in turn can also help in improving the behavior traits of the rest as well.

These Following phrases encourage and reinforce positive behaviors and help build confidence in individuals.

- "Great job following directions!"
- "I love how you're working so hard."
- "You're being so responsible!"
- "Thank you for being a kind friend."
- "You're really improving!"
- "I noticed how you helped without being asked."
- "That was an awesome choice."
- "You stayed so calm. Well done!"

- "You're showing great self-control!"
- "I'm proud of how you handled that."
- "Look at you being a great problem-solver!"
- "Thank you for sharing!"
- "You're making great progress!"
- "I admire your patience."
- "That was very respectful."
- "You're becoming so independent!"
- "Great listening!"
- "You're really focused today!"
- "Look at that teamwork!"
- "That was so helpful of you."
- "Thank you for using kind words."
- "You made a thoughtful choice!"
- "Great perseverance!"
- "You're being a good role model."
- "Excellent effort!"
- "You're a good friend."
- "Look how far you've come!"
- "That was very brave."
- "You showed great empathy."
- "Thank you for being respectful."

- "I can see you're really trying!"
- "What a creative solution!"
- "I'm impressed by your responsibility."
- "That's a big improvement!"

Using Intervention:

A classroom is a teacher's territory and before the teacher can commence with her work of teaching they must habituate themselves with the fact that not every student learns or adapts at the same rate nor they have come from the same background. Sometimes some students may show traits of disruptive and challenging behaviors as well and in those cases the teacher must not be reactive in their response. As mentioned in the framework, on such times the teacher can apply the interventions according to the needs of the students. There must be a universal tier to deal with the class in general but the teacher will have to be supportive and proactive about giving targeted support to the students who are finding it difficult. For example in a class if a couple of students are found weaker in understanding communication cues than an additional assistance should be provided to them by the teachers. These interventions do not bifurcate the classrooms between those who can and those who can not, rather they help in bringing a balance in the learning atmosphere which in long run establishes an equal level of each student.

Promoting Positive Relationship:

Building A strong bond with the students is a pivotal point of PBS. If the teacher needs to control and conduct a classroom according to the set expectations they can not remain cold and formal. They need to foster trust and respect in the students and to create a safe space for the students to feel confident. By creating a space where open communication is welcomed and encouraged the teachers can win the confidence of the children and the classroom will become a place of shared thoughts and ideas. Secondly the teachers can always implement activities to promote teamwork and this collaborative approach will bring an air of unity among the students where they will gradually be equipped with the values of cooperation and mutual help. Lastly the teacher must turn into an active listener. The students should feel heard and valued in the class. If their concerns and worries are being heard with attention and care and being addressed thoughtfully then the underlying issues of particular behavioral challenges can be addressed properly by the teachers.

Nowadays the classroom has become a dynamic and ever changing platform for both the teachers and the students. A fixation on curriculum and mugging up of the syllabus is completely out of the question. Teachers are now required to know not only the syllabus they tackle but must be equipped with tasks to ensure an environment of learning and character building. Under PBS teachers are asked to formulate data-driven decision making particularly in the areas of routine, expectations and consistency.

What is Data in the Education System?

In today's classroom education has become more individualistic where each student's need to be taken care of and to identify those there are parameters including academic performances, behavioral records, attendance data and feedback from students and their guardians. These metrics help teachers to understand the students they are dealing with for a long time of the day, better. These effective use of data allows educators to tailor a teaching method and optimize the classroom routines.

Data to develop Effective Classroom:

First the teachers are needed to pay close attention to identify disruptions made by the students and the times and activities that cause the maximum amount of disruptions . by collecting these data they get a clear idea as to how to revise the routine. For example if a teacher notices a spike in disruption after a particular class or between classes then there must be strategies that can be implemented to make a smooth transition between classes without much disruption. Once the new routine is effective the educators must always seek feedback from the students through indirect or direct surveys to see how helpful the routine has proved to be.

Establishing a coherent set of goals is the next data driven strategy that the teachers can apply in class. If a classroom is getting more disrupted during group assignments then the expectations around collaborative approaches should be set clearly to the students. These expectations must be presented in forms of posters or discussed regularly to be clearly communicated to the students. It is the teacher's responsibility to explicitly clear the expectations to the students so that they don't have an iota of doubt regarding the expectations because only then they can successfully internalize the things expected from them. Finally in the post implementation stage reinforcement of the expectations are vital. Students must feel acknowledged meeting the expectations.

Consistency is the key:

To ensure the success of the PBS the teachers must consider consistency as the most crucial part. This is something that they must learn to do for the fruition of the goals they have set forth. Inconsistency can harm the process or worse the growth of the students as they will become confused and lose interest and motivation in maintaining and following the expectations. Each teacher must take on a balanced approach to maintain the consistency of the class through regular monitoring and collection of data to see any lapse or improvement. The process of regular data collection can also help a teacher in acquiring any additional assistance. In such cases professional helps become vital and much effective who target the particular area that needs a revision or alteration. In the PBS system each teacher or educator needs to be in alignment when it comes to their effort to bring a positive learning environment for the students.

By using data in a classroom to ameliorate the existent routine, expectation and practicing them with consistency can smooth the process of implementing PBS. If students are being motivated to work in collaboration and encouraged to be accountable, their same rule is applied to the teachers as well because, after all, they are the mediators, the models that would guide the students. There must be responsibility among the colleagues in creating a collaborative approach towards building an effective classroom. Ultimately PBS does not work on students exclusively and teachers and educators do have a vital role in it as implementers and as a subject of it as well.

Chapter-8: Role of Teachers in Positive Behaviour Support

As already discussed in the previous chapters in the dynamic and evolved education system teachers' role has become multidimensional and as the architects of the learning environment the teachers need to be open minded and receptive of any change that they must welcome or craft out on their own. The books and the curriculum set for the academic purpose has turned into one of the many aspects of education and not just the only purpose of education. Teachers are now coming out of the set traditional pattern of teaching and instruction and embracing their roles as a facilitator of positive behavior in the classroom. No longer do we have the blackboard system in schools now digitalization has been spread all over India and maximum schools are getting aid from the government to adapt the new technologies to propagate a modern and effective way of teaching for which the teachers also need to be equipped with the skill to operate. Likewise under the modern thought process educators need to be a medium of cultivating positive behaviors in students. They need proper structural training on this and a constructive evaluation to build themselves as models to implement those positive traits in children. Teachers play a critical role in forecasting and supporting positive student behavior within school environments. As the primary adults interacting with students on a daily basis, teachers have unique insights and opportunities to shape and reinforce constructive behaviors.

When we say teachers need to be well equipped it means the teachers must be trained to face challenges in the classroom which includes dealing with disruptive behaviors and learning several proactive strategies instead of reactive ones in order to handle the issues effectively. From building a list of expected behaviors and reinforcing the desirable behaviors through rewards and certification they should work to build a conducive learning atmosphere and must seek help when their set expectations don't seem to fit the class. In the implementation of PBS collaborative efforts of immense significance where a bridge is erected between the school, the students, the parents and the community and in that efforts teachers lead the way. Teachers' role is instrumental in building a supportive, empathetic and respectful relationship among each sector. PBS is not something that can be a one sided effort and every kind of reciprocation becomes vital and teachers facilitate that reciprocative communication between the school and the parents.

Expected Role of Teachers:

- First and foremost, teachers must establish clear behavioral expectations from the outset. This involves collaborating with school administrators to develop and communicate a comprehensive set of rules, consequences, and positive incentives. Consistently enforcing these guidelines helps students understand boundaries and appropriate conduct.

- Beyond setting standards, teachers can proactively forecast potential behavioral challenges. By closely observing student tendencies, emotional states, and environmental triggers, teachers can anticipate situations that may provoke disruptive actions. This foresight allows them to intervene early, redirecting students before problems escalate.

- Equally important is a teacher's ability to model and reinforce positive behaviors. Through their own actions and interactions, teachers demonstrate respectful communication, impulse control, and constructive problem-solving. When students witness these desirable behaviors in their educators, they are more likely to emulate them.
- Furthermore, teachers can capitalize on their rapport with students to provide individualized behavior support. By understanding each young person's unique needs, triggers, and motivations, teachers can craft tailored strategies to help them manage their emotions and actions. This personalized approach fosters trust and self-regulation skills.
- Finally, teachers must partner with parents, administrators, and support staff to create a cohesive behavior management system. Regular communication, data-sharing, and collaborative problem-solving ensure a unified, whole-child approach to positive behavior forecasting and support.

In essence, teachers are on the frontlines of shaping student conduct in school. Through thoughtful planning, modeled behavior, individualized support, and cross-team collaboration, teachers can powerfully forecast and promote positive behaviors that benefit the entire learning community.

Moreover the classroom should not become a place of fear and anxiety for the students and it is the duty of the teachers to maintain the demeanor of a kind and helping individual so that the students can feel safe and supported inside the classroom in the presence of the teacher. But being kind does not mean indulging in the unruly and unacceptable behaviors of the students but being able to find alternatives to reactive measures in order to bring a change in the classroom atmosphere. These targeted behaviors and strategies of the teachers are only possible through training and professional development of the teachers. They must know the behavioral theories, intervention strategies, and restorative practices and get habituated with the nuances of implementing the PBS. A well trained teacher will be able to recognize the early signs of distress and respond appropriately to the challenging situations.

However if the teachers are required to perform in alignment with PBS structure then there are certain checkboxes that must be ticked to ensure the well being of the teachers aw well. a professionally secure and and personally balanced person can carry out the task of creating a well rounded model in front of the students. There are certain personal developments that are required of the teachers in order to expect a change in their way of handling a class. These developments are done on the personal and professional front and are often the responsibility of the school authority to ensure. This chapter will delve into the ways in which the positions of the teachers can be secured so that they can carry out the implementation of PBS efficiently.

Surveys have shown how the process of integrating and implementing the PBS in schools can be a challenging process for the teachers as well. Thus it becomes crucial to manage personal stress and build resilience for educators for effective navigation of these challenges.

The Stress in the Teaching Profession and Significance of Resilience:

Teaching is inherently demanding, often leading to high levels of stress. Factors contributing to this stress include heavy workloads, diverse student needs, administrative pressures, and a lack of resources. PBS, while beneficial, adds another layer of complexity. It requires teachers to adjust their approach, embrace new strategies, and often engage in ongoing professional development. Understanding these stressors is the first step in managing them effectively.

The first step to manage stress would be to prioritize self care and a balanced lifestyle. It is of absolute necessity for a teacher to build the model for the students and thus to be more careful towards the personal development which includes a constructive routine of self care. This schedule can include mindfulness and relaxation tactics such as yoga and follow a more structured and well planned routine which will keep the mind relaxed and free of any anxiety. This positive approach towards the teachers own wellbeing can reflect into the students they will be teaching at class. If the teacher always shows up in a calm demeanor and in enhanced mood and positivity then automatically the same vibration will radiate through the students and the interactions between the teachers and the students will become more effective. Next is professional time management. Either by following the old school planners or applying the digital tools to plan out a day ahead can reduce stress in teachers. It must not be forgotten that in the modern learning structure teachers must carry a lot off responsibilities and struggling with all those duties within a limited time is quite cumbersome if no structure is followed. Thus following a personal or a professional planner would be impactful in preventing stress and exhaustion in teachers. At times this work pressure becomes an inseparable part of their job and in such cases schools must look into the well being of the teachers as the mediator of education and PBS to students.

Another most important aspect of teachers' training is building resilience in them so that they can tackle the challenges effectively and maintain a positive outlook. To empower teachers, schools need to arrange a consistent learning process and professional development for the teachers wherein they can not only acquire necessary skills for PBS but a sense of confidence and competence can foster. Teachers must be encouraged to track their progress as well to realize their shortcomings and improvements. This attitude helps teachers to be grounded and reinforces a growth mindset. Moreover a positive school environment can significantly enhance teacher resilience. Administrators can promote a culture that values collaboration, respect, and open communication. Regular staff meetings to celebrate successes and discuss challenges can foster a sense of belonging and shared purpose among teachers. Sometimes the goals for PBS set by the teachers go too over the board and end up being unachievable; this not only brings a halt in the progress of the strategies but also creates frustration and burnout in teachers. Thus they must be realistic in setting their goals for the PBS framework.

Managing personal stress and building resilience are critical components for teachers implementing Positive Behavior Support in schools. By prioritizing self-care, fostering a supportive school culture, and engaging in continuous professional development, educators can navigate the complexities of PBS more effectively. Through practical strategies and collaborative efforts, teachers can not only enhance their own well-being but also create a positive and conducive learning environment for their students. By cultivating resilience, educators are better equipped to face challenges, celebrate successes, and ultimately thrive in their profession.

Under the PBS framework it is of utmost importance that the teachers must grasp the core elements of the PBS. The success of PBS depends on the professional development of the teachers as they are the primary mediators of the system and they need to be well equipped with the very concept of PBS and skills to implement the PBS effectively. PBS is mainly grounded in the principles of applied behavior analysis and it prioritized proactive prevention of any behavioral issues that arise inside the classroom and look for the support of the community as well. Under professional development, PBS focus falls on understanding the framework's core components: defining, teaching, monitoring, and reinforcing expected behaviors as well as responding to problem behaviors effectively.

Educators and teachers must be well versed in the concept of PBS. The underlying principle of PBS must be very clear to the teachers, including the importance of positive behavior in school and the role of social-emotional learning. They must express their shared values and ideas and also understand their position in this framework as facilitators of the agenda. Through data collection methods teachers should be trained to assess the behaviors of the students. However they can also follow direct observation and behavior rating scales to identify the trigger points of challenging behaviors. Sometimes direct support is provided to the teachers by experienced trainers who observe classrooms and give their feedback. These professionals also assist teachers in refining their implementations. Most importantly educators should be well familiarized with the evidence-based intervention strategies aligning with the PBS. This will help them to understand the plans to adapt in order to develop individualized support plans for students with persistent behavioral issues and using the interventions to meet each student's needs. Teachers must understand that PBS is a collaborative venture and thus they must be trained to engage and involve parents and communities of the students in the process. They are also required to form a collaborative environment of work by maintaining a healthy professional relationship with their colleagues and staff. This will foster a sense of teamwork among the facilitators of the PBS which ensures a consistent distribution of PBS across all grade levels and classrooms.

A continuous investigation of the teachers' professional development bears significant effects on the teachers' methods. Sometimes this builds a sense of confidence in teachers and thereby they feel more at ease in handling the behavior of their students. Once the teacher gains this sense of efficacy they become more involved in the implementation of the PBS with their morale enhanced and also provides them with an increased job satisfaction. The ultimate goal of a teacher is to foster an overall growth and improvement in their students and this endeavor is incomplete without a professional development of the teacher. Alongside the academic development of the children the teachers are now needed to ensure a behavioral improvement in every child and for that they need to feel confident in their behavior management skills. They must know how to deal with challenging behaviors and address the challenging behaviors and create an inclusive learning atmosphere. But all these aspects of professional development are not the responsibility of the teachers alone. They are also a part of the program in which they must be trained to be ready and for that the school authorities should take the charge of providing the needful training and workshop to prepare them for the PBS framework and fully realize the gravity of the matter.

As discussed prior in the chapters, PBS is an elaborated process and neither happens in a fortnight nor can be carried out by just distributing some pamphlets. It's an elongated process that involves a deeper understanding of the process and maintaining the consistency and dedication in reaching the completion. Therefore an engagement of every level of the school is essential: from school authority to the teachers, from students to their parents and community every single person must be brought under the influence of PBS and this work of medium is the teacher. The teachers meditate on the process of PBS for which the schools must take the lead to prepare them for the process and the end goal.

Chapter-9: Applying Positive Behaviour Support for Challenging Behaviors and Special Students

The art of handling challenging behaviors is the key criteria of PBS. And first it is needed from the school and the teachers to understand the children's behaviors, understanding the issues that may be affecting how and why they are acting in such a manner in the class. Teachers need to ask them regarding any issues that may be creating some difficulty for them with the classroom situation or if it is something outside the classroom. Once the teachers get a clear idea about these aspects only then they can begin a wise and effective responsive action. In the process of understanding the children's behavior there are a bunch of questions that formulate a structure of understanding the situations better:

1. Is there an issue with the subject matter?

Children often misbehave in the class if the subject is too hard for them or if it's too easy and in both cases they get bored and disinterested if the teaching style doesn't suit their learning.

2. Is the child emotionally motivated?

Children do misbehave if they are seeking attention or want to feel in-control or at times as a reaction to perceived hurt or injustice. At times their behavior spurs out from a fear of failure and to cover up if they feel inadequate.

3. Is there a problem at school?

Often a child who has been bullied gets traumatized and in reaction becomes fearful, anxious and withdrawn from the class. Some may act out in the form of bullying and others become reclusive and refuse any participation. This is also an emotional problem in children when they want to impose the same that they have felt onto others.

4. Does behavior reflect socio-economic issues?

The home environment affects a child's learning and their behavior severely. Surveys have shown how a child with a healthy home atmosphere tends to be more well behaved and attentive in class than the ones who carry out several responsibilities at home and their attention gets dispersed. For example if the children have an ill family member at home or if there is a scarcity of basic needs, they find it difficult to keep a free mind to participate in the class.

5. Is there any medical or biological issue?

Feeling unwell or depressed, for example, influences how children behave. It's normal for children to occasionally forget their homework, daydream during class, act without thinking, or get fidgety, but there can be some underlying health issues linked to attention deficit disorder (ADD), sometimes also called attention deficit hyperactivity disorder (ADHD). Children who struggle to read and spell could have dyslexia, which affects the way in which the brain recognises and processes symbols, or some other learning difficulty. Hearing and vision problems can also contribute to poor behavior.

Thus it becomes important for the educators to conduct a one-on-one meeting and discussion with the parents of the child more often or whenever they detect any such signs in the children. For the educators it's needed not to bring any temporary remedy but to delve into the bottom of the issue. Understanding the context and circumstances that shape learners' behavior will not only point to solutions, it can also prevent unfair punishments, which often feeds an ongoing cycle of anger, resentment and disruptive behavior. Other than that the teachers can follow certain strategies to respond to the challenging behaviors in the classroom.

Challenging Behavior	Ways to Respond
Attention Seeking	Redirecting the towards more positive behavior
	Reminding them of the task and give them potential choices
	Only giving attention when they are behaving well
Showing Power	Contending the child's power or compromising makes the child eager to test their power in the future.
	Staying calm
	Trying to understand their feelings and showing that the educators or teachers understand their feeling

	Helping the child in understanding that they can use their power for a better cause and more constructively
Revenge	Being patient is the best strategy. Punishment can worsen the case as they would become more eager to become resentful
	A friendly approach helps the child to cool down faster
	Encouraging the child that they will be respected if they give the same back.
Inadequacy	Criticizing should not be practiced
	Arranging for extra classes to improve the child's learning and also breaking lessons into small parts for their benefit
	Encouraging children to focus on their improvements and success rather than comparing small achievements with others'.

Source: Paul Vietnam, 2009

It is true that handling difficult behaviors in class, especially the recurring and adamant ones, is a toll on the calm of the teachers but in no case scenarios the teachers are advised to practice negative disciplines in PBS. The negative discipline includes: commanding, forbidding, criticizing, threatening, and unreasonable punishments.

- Commanding: "Go over there and sit down!"
- Forbidding: "Stop that!" "Don't touch that!" "Don't do it like that!"
- Criticizing: "You are going to break that"
- Belittling: "When are you going to get it right?" "When are you going to learn to do what I say?"
- Threatening: "I will send you to the Principal's office!" "You are going to be in so much trouble"
- Unreasonable punishments: "You are going to stand in the corner for the whole day!" "I am giving you detention for the whole month!"

Teachers often take the authoritative stand in the class and impose certain punishments that add to the embarrassment and shame of the students and in future encourage the challenging behaviors.

Applying PBS for Special Children:

For students with special needs such as autism, ADHD or other intellectual disabilities, PBS offers a structured and individualized strategy to promote social, academic and emotional growth. In the case of the special education system it's important to create visual schedules and provide reliable routines for students. Students with autism often benefit from visual cues that help in their understanding. If they are given a structured atmosphere they feel more at ease and this reduces their anxiety also. Under PBS students with special needs are often provided individualized support. They need tailored interventions based on their unique needs, strengths, and challenges. In such cases educators must provide them with Functional Behaviour Assessment (FBAs) to detect and identify the root cause of a particular behavioral issues such as communication difficulties or sensory overload. After such assessments teachers can tailor a more suitable and personalized intervention to cater to the specific needs of the children. A student who may have an issue with frustration must be taught self-regulation through breathing techniques and other meditative activities and must not be punished for showing any misbehavior.

To address behavioral challenges, identifying underlying causes and to create an effective intervention the educators need to follow a more personalized approach which can be achieved by using the support tools like Individual Behaviour Plans (IBPs) and Functional Behaviour Assessment (FBAs). These two are often combined with Tiered Support Systems like Response To Intervention (RTI) and Multi-Tiered System of Support (MTSS) and they provide a holistic and data-driven approach to behavior management and academic success in special students.

Individual Behaviour Plans (IBPs):

It is a customized strategy designed for students with specific needs. Under this plan teachers can teach appropriate goals to the students for developing positive behaviors in them and also reinforcing desired actions and also addressing areas where the students may struggle such as impulse control and communication skills. The component of IBF includes:

Clear and Measurable goals	Intervention Strategies	Reinforcement Systems	Regular Monitoring and adjustment

Functional Behaviour Assessment (FBAs):

It is a critical process that helps in determining the root cause of students' behaviors. It includes observing the student, collecting data on behavior patterns, and analyzing the environment to understand triggers or motivations. If a student is having issues with attention and it is the root cause of their disruptive behavior which is also causing difficulty with academics and sensory sensitivities, then the detection of the underlying cause of attention must be understood to design a targeted intervention that will address the particular need of the student. FBA typically involves:

Identifying the target behavior	Collecting Data	Analyzing Pattern	Developing and intervention Plan

Tiered support Systems: RTI and MTSS

Unlike IBPs and FBA, Response to Intervention and Multi-tiered System of Support offer a broader framework for academic and behavioral support as per their needs.

RTI: It is an approach that focuses on providing early and evidence-based interventions to struggling students. In RTI there are mainly three tiers:

TIER-1	Universal interventions that are provided to all students in the general education classroom, such as high-quality instruction and behavior management strategies.
TIER-2	Targeted interventions for students who need more support than what is provided in Tier 1. These students may receive small-group instruction or specialized behavioral interventions.
TIER-3	Intensive, individualized interventions for students with significant needs. At this stage, students may receive one-on-one support, including individualized behavior plans and tailored academic assistance.

MTSS: It provides a more unified and comprehensive framework for both academic and behavorial development of students. This approach addresses the child's every need combining RTIfor academic concerns and also behavioral support systems. Like RTI MTSS also works a three tiered model:

TIER-1	Providing universal and evidence based instructions for behavioral support
TIER-2	Giving targeted interventions to students who are at risk of developing some academic or behavioral challenges

TIER-3	Giving a more individualized support to students with some significant challenges. Like students with ADHD, or autism or some sensory sensitivity

The behavior management of special students is a collaborative effort where special support is needed from special educators, parents and therapists. To create the environment for the holistic development of these students the support system must work like a team across different areas- home, school, and therapy settings.

In the school setting students with issues can have support from special educators who are specialized in training and managing classroom behaviors and implementing individualized intervention as per the needs of the students. They are specialized in creating Individualized Education Plans to provide structured routines and implementing strategies such as FBAs. They also carry out the crucial task of observing students' responses. Next is the role of parents who are the most crucial part of fostering positive behavior outside the school because they know the child's trigger and coping mechanisms better than the educators. The task of maintaining consistency across the environment of school befalls them. By regularly communicating with the educators and establishing a bond with the child the parents can make the child feel confident and safe and also prepare them for the school. Finally the therapist also forms a crucial part in the students' support system. Therapists like speech-language pathologists, occupational therapists, and behavior analysts, use their expertise and medical methods in identifying the root cause of the child's challenging behaviors. For example a child with communication difficulties and is suffering from behavioral outburst can be benefitted from a speech therapist. Therapists often work in collaboration with parents and educators to cater to the particular and unique needs of the student more effectively.

In essence PBS weaves a personalized road map for the special students by delving deep into the root cause of the challenging behavior. PBS also equips the students with essential life skills through a powerful synergy of educators, parents and therapists. This kind of approach not only creates a strong unified support system but also enables the students with a safe space where they can face their limitations or issues and work towards curing them. Thus PBS is not just a mere strategy but a tool to empower the students for a bright and better future ahead.

Chapter-10: Evaluating Sustaining PBS in Schools And Positive Behaviour Support Policy Advocacy in India

We have come all the way in understanding the importance of PBS as a vital part of the curriculum in schools. PBS has come a long way since its humble beginning as a nonprofit broadcaster to its role as a trusted source of education, entertainment, and public service, PBS has continually adapted to meet the evolving needs of its audience. But it's of equal necessity to ensure sustainability of PBS in schools through monitoring and using data and also by adapting long term strategies for sustainability. It is pertinent that PBS stays active in every school environment of the Indian education system. It must not remain as an urban approach rather must reach out gradually to the distant borders of the country.

PBS is an ongoing process that needs to be constantly regulated and monitored. Only by monitoring progress and outcomes the workings of the system can be reflected upon as well as the areas of further improvement can emerge. By systematically collecting data on student behaviour, academic performance, and overall school climate, educators can make informed decisions about the effectiveness of their strategies. Equally a flexible data-driven approach allows schools to tailor interventions as per the varied needs of the students and ensure that behavior support systems should remain impactful and more reliable over time. Finally sustainability is the key to achieve a smooth path for PBS to reach its full potential in bringing a change in the school scenario of india. The insights here aim to guide schools in creating lasting, positive transformations in student behaviour and school culture.

A key component of any successful Positive Behaviour System (PBS) implementation is tracking results and progress, which enables schools to evaluate the effectiveness of their tactics and make appropriate modifications. Continuous monitoring guarantees that programs stay applicable and successful in Indian schools, where varied student populations and sociocultural circumstances frequently pose difficulties.

Monitoring is a key element of evaluation and assessment in a classroom under the PBS curriculum. The monitoring process involves collecting and analyzing data to track the impact of interventions and in making data-driven decisions. The monitoring process must follow these steps to ensure more effective and advanced evaluation of the prevalent process.

DATA COLLECTION	DATA ANALYSIS
Frequency & Duration: in collecting data the temporal aspect of the task or behaviour is the key point. For example when I child shows attention deficit behaviour for a further study on their condition, first the mentor must track the times they left their	**Visual Representation:** to track the progress over a given time the educators and teachers can take help of graphs or charts as visual representation of the progress that has taken place or could be achieved. Making a visual representation also helps in maintaining a structured

seats while doing a task or studying	blueprint of the whole process.
Intensity: measuring the intensity of a particular behaviour is also a crucial piece of monitoring. If the school is dealing with a student who is suffering from anger and aggression issues and in order to address this problem it is important to rate the intensity of the behaviour.	**Data-Based Decision Making:** not only just keeping track of the behaviours but it is also important to keep a note of the implementations of interventions. The teachers must always go back to assessing the effect of interventions in students through data analysis and make sure to bring change in implementation when required.
Quality: if a child is showing alternative behaviour in class, for instance by interrupting the class if they are raising their hands before speaking , then the quality of such replacement must be evaluated.	A teacher implements a positive behavior intervention plan for a student with disruptive behavior. The teacher tracks the frequency of disruptive incidents, the student's participation in class activities, and the quality of their interactions with

	peers. By analyzing this data, the teacher can determine if the intervention is effective and make adjustments as needed.

Other than data collection and analysis there are several other aspects of monitoring that can be taken into consideration. When the school is taking up the interventions to cater to the needs of the students they must collaborate with the family and peers of the students to get a broad spectrum of insight which will ultimately make the monitoring process more meaningful and relevant. It is always important for the school not to narrow down the observation or limit the process within the walls of the classroom. In order to do so the educators must not rely on a one time report but keep a constant direct observation and also to gather more inputs from the students family.

To ensure the long-term sustainability of Positive Behavioral Interventions and Supports (PBIS) in schools, it's essential to develop a comprehensive framework that emphasizes leadership commitment, staff development, community engagement, and data-driven decision-making. The ultimate goal is to embed PBIS into the school culture so that it becomes a sustainable, integral part of the school's operations.

Leadership commitment is pertinent in the PBS structure because it ensures resource allocating, staff development and school-wide implementation. To maintain a strong momentum and secure necessary resources for implementation the schools need a strong leadership commitment. The school leaders must know the framework of PBS and at the same time ensure that the agenda is getting clearly communicated to the staff, which includes defining their roles, responsibilities and consistent data collection practices. Researches and surveys have shown that when a strong leadership is provided the schools can achieve and sustain PBS for a longer period of time. Moreover the whole process of implementing PBS at school needs a stable funding system and with a strong leader the resources can be utilized properly.

The staffs must be made involved in the process of PBS by offering regular opportunities for training and support through coaching, peer collaboration, and feedback loops ensures that staff remain skilled and motivated to implement PBIS practices consistently.Under the PBS framework staffs are required to have a proper comprehensive training on PBS principles, behavorial analysis and intervention strategies. Therefore the ongoing professional development of the staff becomes equally important in addressing the evolving challenges and to maintain their engagement.

According to Greenberg in PBS a unified approach is vital and that can be guaranteed by a collaboration and multidisciplinary approach to the implementation where school, teachers, family, peers, and mental health care professionals must work together to cater to the specific needs of the students. Engaging families ensures that behavioral expectations are reinforced at home, and collaborating with local organizations can provide supplementary resources.

As discussed earlier the data collection and analysis phase is another aspect of maintaining PBS for a longer time. Assessment of behaviours and tracking measures and implementations allows a door for rectification, alternation and amelioration which in the long run strengthen the program and finally succession planning and evaluation make sure that PBS is not implemented but also is improved more frequently to suit the growing and evolved need of the students. While implementation is a task of perseverance and dedication, maintaining it requires a constant assessment and evaluation to find scopes for improvement and refine strategies accordingly.

Encouraging the inclusion of Positive Behavioural Interventions and Supports (PBIS) in Indian schools is crucial to fostering a nurturing and supportive learning environment. PBIS is an evidence-based framework that promotes positive behavior, improves academic outcomes, and enhances social skills among students. To successfully integrate PBIS into Indian schools, a few key policies and strategies are needed.

On an international level this idea of making PBS a vital section of the curriculum has been taken up long ago. The Positive Behavioural Interventions and Supports (PBIS) has brought the discussion of race, racism with the students for understanding their take on these issues. Moreover in 1998 under the accreditation of National Commission for Certifying Agencies (NCCA) BACB or Behaviour Analyst Certification Board was established and has been leading behaviour analyst certifications for over two decades.the Western Cape Government has also taken initiative to promote positive behaviour in children and youth through their programmes.The Association for Positive Behaviour Support or APBS is another multi disciplinary organisation made up of professionals like teachers, professors, researchers and also family members, and consumers who are committed to the application of PBS within the context of schools, family, community, and also individuals with complex needs for support. The United Kingdom has demonstrated their interest in promoting a positive behaviour system and also addressing challenging behaviour in school students and young adults with organisations like The Challenging Behaviour Foundation.

In India in recent times many such endeavours have been taken into account and they have been working to dissolve the barriers in the learning process of the learners. The International Baccalaureate has aimed to develop a group of inquiring, knowledgeable and caring young people who would contribute in the formation of a better and more peaceful society. To this end the organisation has been working with schools and other educational institutions to develop challenging programs and rigorous assessment. The Indian Public School has brought their inclusive policy in schools wherein value was given to the diverse school culture and also equality was promoted. TIPS has made sure that students with or without special learning needs will be given the right support and space to express themselves. They made it the schools' responsibility to ensure the safety of each child from harm and negligence and the schools must also ensure that our stakeholders are aware of and contribute to the inclusion policy and take up their roles towards achieving it and contribute to the inclusion policy and are aware of individual's role towards. The school has facilities to support students with mild conditions. We are not equipped to handle extreme conditions. In recent years in India both national and local level efforts were made in adapting the PBS framework by the schools and the government. Such of that kind are listed below.

NATIONAL INITIATIVES	
1. National Curriculum Framework (NCF)	The NCF, developed by the National Council of Educational Research and Training (NCERT), encourages a shift from traditional disciplinary methods to more constructive and student-centered approaches. The framework advocates for the holistic development of children, promoting emotional well-being, social skills, and positive behavior, which aligns with PBS principles.

2.	Samagra Shiksha Abhiyan (SSA)	Launched by the Ministry of Education, Samagra Shiksha Abhiyan is an umbrella program for the education of children across India. It focuses on inclusive education, aiming to improve the quality of education for all students, including those with disabilities. This initiative indirectly supports PBS by emphasizing a positive, inclusive school environment, teacher training, and the promotion of social and emotional learning.
3.	National Mental Health Programme (NMHP)	The NMHP has been promoting mental health and well-being in schools. Schools are encouraged to adopt psychosocial support frameworks and create positive environments where students' emotional and social needs are addressed — essential elements of PBS.

4. Atal Tinkering Labs (ATL)	This initiative by the Atal Innovation Mission (AIM) encourages creative thinking and innovation among students. It helps to foster a positive and participatory learning environment, indirectly supporting the development of positive behaviors like collaboration, problem-solving, and critical thinking.

LOCAL INITIATIVES	
1. Delhi's 'School Positive Climate' Program:	In collaboration with UNICEF, Delhi introduced a program to improve the school climate by promoting positive behavior, respect, and inclusivity. This program includes workshops and training for teachers, focusing on creating supportive classroom environments and fostering

	positive behavior in students.
2. The 'Safer Schools' Initiative by UNICEF India:	Aimed at improving child safety and mental health, this initiative supports schools in creating a positive atmosphere by promoting anti-bullying programs and social-emotional learning. It encourages the development of a supportive and non-violent school culture, aligning with PBS values.
3. Karnataka's 'Namma Ooru Namma School' (Our City, Our School):	This local initiative encourages community engagement in schools, aiming to create a positive school culture by involving parents, teachers, and students. It emphasizes the importance of social-emotional learning and

	positive behavior as part of the overall educational experience.

These initiatives that have just started to take shape in our country's education sector are like the initial steps of a big venture. These efforts, if taken up serious monitoring and assessment, can bear the fruit of a bright future for the young and the coming generations.

Conclusion

As we have reached the end of our journey in understanding PBS and its importance in the school curriculum we can consider that knowing about PBS and practicing it are two completely different approaches to it. Our understanding of the book allows us the gateway to a future where Indian schools will not just remain as centres of academic learning but become sanctuaries where positive behavior and emotional well-being will foster. The journey that has been taken up by the readers of this book will find an illuminated path in front of them where the education system of the country will become more inclusive, empathetic and empowering, where the barriers of society, economy, and culture will be nullified and a renewed sense of unity will become the strength of the youth. The journey through the chapters has made it clear that the root of such a change takes form in the classrooms across the country, nurturing a culture of mutual respect, cooperation, and shared responsibility. But as adults, educators, teachers, and parents we know that the path to change is never linear. It is filled with hurdles and victory is only possible through consistent patience and persistence. In the heart of India's bustling classrooms lies an opportunity for revolutionary change – the opportunity to move beyond punitive systems that focus on what is wrong, and instead focus on what is right. Under PBS reprimands need to be altered with rewards and isolation with inclusion. Teaching must be compassionate and respectful. The grades will still be the end goal but it should not be the only goal of a person's academic life.

The case studies, policies, and examples shared within these pages should serve as both inspiration and a call to action. From the success stories in Delhi to local initiatives in Karnataka, we've witnessed how schools across India are beginning to integrate PBS in ways that are culturally resonant, context-specific, and deeply impactful. The power of collaboration has never been clearer – when teachers, students, parents, and communities come together with a shared vision, they can create spaces where positive behaviour is not just encouraged, but expected.

The responsibility to bring about this change does not fall on any one person or organization. In order to achieve a long-term result the whole system of a country must realize the importance of such a framework in making our children more successful in their lives. This book ends here with a note and a hope that the message would reach the ears of all those who are responsible or involved with the education sectors. They might be able to distinguish the current state of education with the probable aftermath of embracing PBS at Indian schools. PBS is not just a structure of instruction but it is the key to fostering a healthy society for the future where students' potentials will be unlocked by positivity, mutual respect and support.

About the Author

Psychology teaches us that the environment we grow up in profoundly shapes who we become, whether at school or home. For me, Naidu Sir was a core component of that environment. He was much more than just a teacher—he was a mentor, a guide, and a source of unwavering support.

The words spoken to a child—and, more importantly, the tone in which they are delivered—are crucial, especially when the child is making mistakes or learning something new. Naidu Sir understood this deeply. Even when I struggled to grasp certain concepts, he never resorted to harshness or criticism. Instead, he used kind and encouraging words that made me feel capable rather than inadequate. He was straightforward yet reassuring, creating an environment that was optimistic and stress-free—far from the high-pressure situations that often overwhelm students.

I came to realise just how important a teacher's role is, especially during formative years. They have the power to either build a child's confidence or shatter it. I used to experience exam anxiety and was often incredibly hard on myself, but Naidu Sir's calm demeanour and reassuring smile became a source of peace and comfort for me.

A teacher, after all, wears many hats: they are mentors, friends, parent figures, emotional anchors, and role models. For me, Naidu Sir embodied all of these roles effortlessly, leaving an indelible impact on my life that I will always carry with me.

Nidhi & Yash

Saher

Since a young age, Naidu Sir has been much more than just a teacher to me—he's been a constant form of support and belief in my life. His unique methods and unwavering support in helping me reach my potential has shaped how I learn and how I view challenges and growth.

What sets him apart are his unconventional approach to teaching. He doesn't rely on rote learning or traditional techniques; instead, he introduces concepts in ways that spark curiosity and make learning an engaging experience. He believes in understanding the topic rather than blindly memorizing it, and this perspective has completely changed how I approach academics.

Beyond academics, Naidu Sir has taught me some of the most valuable life lessons. His patience and ability to turn my mistakes into stepping stones for improvement have shown me the importance of resilience. He never gave in to frustration when I struggled but encouraged me to keep trying, reminding me that every challenge is an opportunity to grow.

Naidu sir, in my eyes, is the definition of "You are never too old to set another goal or to dream a new dream." - a quote by C.S Lewis. Sir's persistence and determination to always search for more and find meaning to life motivates me to do the same. He has a certain spark and drive to achieve more and influence young minds. He is, and always will be, a figure of immense inspiration and guidance in my journey.

Disha

How many can say that my teacher taught my children as well? During my school years Naidu sir was persistent, strict and on point but now when I see him with my children, he is a friend, a confidant and more importantly a mentor to them. He has definitely changed with times and that is a symbol of his ever-evolving personality which inspire us as a whole family. He has also pushed me to start my business and gives me inputs every now and then. Naidu sir has guided me almost my entire life and I am eternally grateful to him.

Vitesha , Ariha & Tanisha :

Naidu Sir is truly an inspiring educator. His passion for learning is infectious, and he has a unique ability to make even the most complex concepts seem accessible and engaging. I particularly appreciate his patience and the way he makes learning easy. He creates a supportive and inclusive learning environment where I feel comfortable asking questions and exploring different perspectives. Naidu sir's enthusiasm for teaching has not only deepened my understanding but also ignited my own intellectual curiosity

Message
LOVE AND CARE FOR ANIMALS

Dazy.

www.ingramcontent.com/pod-product-compliance
Lightning Source LLC
LaVergne TN
LVHW061619070526
838199LV00078B/7338